LUCENT LIBRARY *of* HISTORICAL ERAS

PEOPLES AND EMPIRES OF ANCIENT MESOPOTAMIA

DON NARDO

LUCENT BOOKS

A part of Gale, Cengage Learning

GALE
CENGAGE Learning™

Detroit • New York • San Francisco • New Haven, Conn • Waterville, Maine • London

GALE
CENGAGE Learning

LIBRARY OF CONGRESS CATALOGING-IN-PUBLICATION DATA

Nardo, Don, 1947–
  Peoples and empires of ancient Mesopotamia / by Don Nardo.
    p. cm. — (The Lucent library of historical eras)
  Includes bibliographical references and index.
  ISBN 978-1-4205-0101-8 (hardcover)
  1. Iraq—History—To 634—Juvenile literature. I. Title.
  DS71.N372 2008
  935—dc22
                                                          2008015334

Lucent Books
27500 Drake Rd.
Farmington Hills, MI 48331

ISBN-13: 978-1-4205-0101-8
ISBN-10: 1-4205-0101-1

Printed in the United States of America
2 3 4 5 6 7 13 12 11 10 09

Contents

Foreword

Looking back from the vantage point of the present, history can be viewed as a myriad of intertwining roads paved by human events. Some paths stand out—broad highways whose mileposts, even from a distance of centuries, are clear. The events that propelled the rise to power of Germany's Third Reich, its role in World War II, and its eventual demise, for example, are well defined and documented.

Other roads are less distinct, their route sometimes hidden from view. Modern legislatures may have developed from old tribal councils, for example, but the links between them are indistinct in places, open to discussion and interpretation.

The architecture of civilization—law, religion, art, science, and government—as well as the more everyday aspects of our culture—what we eat, what we wear—all developed along the historical roads and byways. In that progression can be traced every facet of modern life.

A broad look back along these roads reveals that many paths—though of vastly different character—seem to converge at a few critical junctions. These intersections are those great historical eras that echo over the long, steady course of human history, extending beyond the past and into the present.

These epic periods of time are the focus of Historical Eras. They shine through the mists of history like beacons, illuminated by a burst of creativity that propels events forward—so bright that we, from thousands of years away, can clearly see the chain of events leading to the present.

Each Historical Eras consists of a set of books that highlight various aspects of these major eras. For example, the Elizabethan England library features volumes on Queen Elizabeth I and her court, Elizabethan theater, the great playwrights, and everyday life in Elizabethan London.

The mini-library approach allows for the division of each era into its most significant and most interesting parts and the exploration of those parts in depth. Also, social and cultural trends as well as illustrative documents and eyewitness accounts can be prominently featured in individual volumes.

Historical Eras presents a wealth of information to young readers. The lively narrative, fully documented primary and secondary source quotations, maps, photographs, sidebars, and annotated bibliographies serve as launching points for class discussion and further research.

In studying the great historical eras, students also develop a better understanding of our own times. What we learn from the past and how we apply it in the present may shape the future and may determine whether our era will be a guiding light to those traveling future roads.

Introduction

On Civilization's Cutting Edge

Today, many people living in Western countries, including the United States and the nations of Europe, look on the Middle East as a somewhat mysterious and at times troubled region. (The Middle East encompasses Egypt, Lebanon, Syria, Iraq, Iran, Saudi Arabia, and some of their immediate neighbors.) They see most of the peoples of that region as having somewhat exotic or odd customs and ideas, at least by Western standards. In particular, Westerners associate the Middle East with the Islamic religion and with a small but active group of Islamic extremists who oppose and sometimes attack the West.

Partly because of such images of the Middle East as a sort of world apart, large numbers of Westerners do not realize the cultural debt they owe to earlier civilizations that occupied that region. Scholars refer to the Middle East before the modern era as the Near East. And at the heart of the ancient Near East lay Mesopotamia, roughly encompassing what is now Iraq. The word originally meant "the land between the rivers," a reference to the Tigris and Euphrates, which flow across Iraq and empty into the Persian Gulf. It was here that the earliest of the four so-called cradles of civilization was located. (The other three were in Egypt, India, and China.)

A Host of Innovations

Indeed, the importance of ancient Mesopotamia to later world cultures cannot be overstated. Some five thousands years ago, the people who inhabited the region stood at the forefront, or cutting edge, of developing human civilization. In the words of the late, great historian Samuel N. Kramer, that people, the Sumerians,

developed the world's earliest true civilization from roots extending far back into the dimness of prehistory. It was Mesopotamia that saw the rise of man's first urban centers, with their rich, complex, and varied life, where political loyalty was no longer to the tribe or clan but to the community as a whole; where lofty ziggurats, or temple-towers, rose skyward, filling the citizen's heart with awe, wonder and pride; where art and technological ingenuity, industrial specialization and commercial enterprise found room to grow and expand.[1]

In was also in these earliest human cities that people first invented writing. This had profound effects on education;

the collection and spread of knowledge, art, and other cultural developments; and trade and other economic activities. In addition, the region witnessed a host of other innovations. Among the more important were the emergence of the first law codes, the earliest complex religious institutions, and the world's first standing armies. With these armies, Sumerian kings became the world's first imperialists (leaders or nations that try to impose their wills on other nations).

Effects on Later Cultures

These advances and developments did not remain localized in the Sumerian

Mesopotamia sits at the heart of the ancient Near East, roughly occupying what is now Iraq.

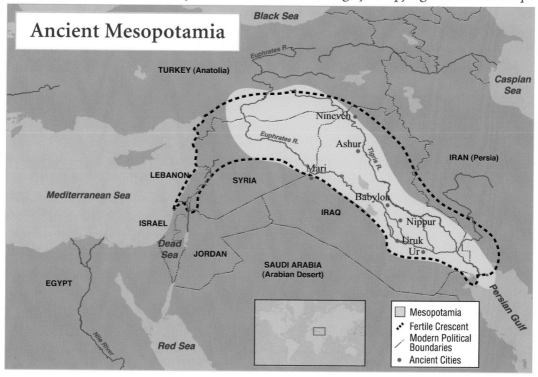

heartland. Instead, over time they spread outward to other parts of Mesopotamia, and from there into neighboring regions. They "had far-reaching effects on economic, intellectual, and cultural progress" in those regions, Kramer says.

Ideas, techniques, and inventions originated by the Sumerians and nurtured by later Mesopotamian peoples . . . were diffused east and west to leave their mark on practically all the cultures of antiquity [ancient times] and even on those of our own day. . . . Kingship—the notion that a ruler's right to rule was bestowed by the gods . . . passed into the very fiber of Western society . . . [and] Mesopotamian law shed its light over much of the civilized world. Greece and Rome were influenced by it through their contacts with the Near East, and Islam acquired a formal legal code only after it had conquered the region that is now Iraq.[2]

Thus, the relatively small area lying along the northwestern edge of the Persian Gulf had a major influence on later human cultures everywhere.

Reconstructing Mesopotamia

In examining the highly influential civilization of ancient Mesopotamia, it is fitting to begin with the peoples who fashioned that civilization. In addition to the Sumerians and their immediate ancestors, they included the Akkadians, Elamites, Babylonians, Assyrians, Medes, Persians, Greeks, Parthians, Sassanians, Arabs, and many others. In their turn, they rose to and fell from prominence in the region during the long period that delineates ancient Mesopotamia—roughly 3300 B.C. to the seventh century A.D.

Very little of a concrete nature has survived about the personalities and achievements of average individuals within these ancient Mesopotamian groups. But archaeologists and historians have amassed a fair amount of information about their rulers and the cities, city-states, political institutions, laws, and empires they fashioned. This allows for a partial and necessarily sweeping, though fascinating, reconstruction of ancient Mesopotamian history.

The reason this history must remain partial is that large gaps remain in the ancient records. Some were destroyed over time by the weather, natural disasters, and wars and other human activities. Others have yet to be found. It is also important to note that these records were never complete or comprehensive to begin with. With a few exceptions (mostly Greeks born long after the Akkadian, Assyrian, and Babylonian empires had fallen), the peoples of the region did not write systematic, detailed histories. So facts about them often must be pieced together from scattered religious writings, sculptures showing exploits by individual kings, and various other writings and artifacts accidentally uncovered by archaeologists.

Carvings of dragons adorn a wall from the gates of Ishtar at Babylon, constructed during the time of Nebuchadnezzar II. Large gaps occur in the ancient records of Mesopotamia, so facts about this time period must be pieced together from writings, sculptures, and artifacts uncovered by archaeologists.

Thus, as University of Michigan scholar Stephen Bertman points out, reconstructing ancient Mesopotamia's history "won't be easy." However, he adds, "the journey must be undertaken, for at stake is our understanding of how one of the earliest of human civilizations assumed an organizational form that enabled it to achieve great things, some of which—like urban life, law, and imperialism—became, for better or worse, its legacy to our times."[3]

Chapter One

The First Farmers and City Dwellers

Thousands of years ago, Mesopotamia and the lands lying along its western and northern rim witnessed two pivotal turning points in the long saga of human civilization. These were the rise of agriculture and the creation of the first cities. The world's first farmers lived in a wide area of foothills that contained numerous fertile valleys. It stretched from southern Palestine (bordering the eastern coast of the Mediterranean Sea), northward through Syria, and across the northern rim of the Mesopotamian plains (what is now Iraq). Modern scholars came to call this semicircular zone of rich farmlands the Fertile Crescent. It remains unclear who the earliest residents of the Fertile Crescent were and where they came from. More certain is that they underwent a transition from hunting and gathering to farming around 9000 B.C. or somewhat earlier.

This change in the way people acquired food was crucial to the later development of human society. For untold generations, they had moved from region to region, following migrating animal herds and living off the land. Now, as farmers, they had permanent, reliable food sources that allowed them to remain in one area. There, they could build settlements, which became the world's first villages.

Stable food sources also promoted increases in population. Eventually, some of these early agriculturists moved eastward and southward into the Mesopotamian plains. And as local populations continued to grow, the world's first cities appeared on those plains. With these cities came local governments and rulers, large public buildings, arts and crafts, trade, rivalries, wars, and other traits, good and bad, that have characterized human civilization ever since.

Early Farms and Villages

The rise of cities, kings, public structures, and so forth in Mesopotamia would have been impossible without the farming traditions established in the Fertile Crescent millennia before. In the initial centuries of the agricultural revolution, farmers developed the earliest forms of the crops that would later become staples in Mesopotamia. These included barley, emmer wheat, flax, chickpeas, lentils, garlic, cucumbers, lettuce, apples, figs, and grapes. Of these, barley, a salt-tolerant kind of wheat, was a particularly important nutritional source. People used the barley kernels to make a thick porridge. They also learned to grind them up into flour to make a flat bread, which is still popular across the Middle East.

The occupants of the Fertile Crescent also raised domesticated animals. Among them were oxen, used for plowing and eating, as well as cattle, sheep, donkeys, goats, pigs, ducks, and geese. Sheep were probably the most numerous of these animals. In addition to their value as a food source, they produced wool, which people learned to transform into yarn for making clothes. Farmers usually moved their flocks of sheep and goats from pasture to

The farming traditions established in the Fertile Crescent paved the way for farming in Mesopotamia. Shown here is a sickle used for farming, made between 4000 and 3500 B.C.

Early Farming Tools and Techniques

Ancient Mesopotamian farmers used mostly wooden implements. Among them were wooden plows pulled by oxen, metal-tipped axes mounted on wooden handles, and wooden sickles with sharpened flint blades attached to them. The sickles were used to cut down wheat and other crops. At planting time in the third millennium B.C., a farmhand followed the plow, sprinkling seeds into the furrows the plow had dug up. Sometime in the next millennium, however, someone invented a plow with a vertical funnel attached. With it, the farmer filled the funnel with seeds, which dropped down into the furrows as the oxen pulled the plow along. Planting time was generally in the fall or early winter, while farmers harvested their crops in April or May.

pasture. In contrast, they kept their cattle and pigs in pens year-round. The cattle were especially important. These large beasts not only produced both meat and milk, they also became offerings to the gods in religious rituals.

Because farmers needed to tend their crops and animals from season to season, it was necessary to maintain permanent settlements. Historians think that by around 7000 B.C., small villages—each consisting of a few crude thatch or mud-brick huts—were common throughout the Fertile Crescent. Two surviving examples are Qalat Jarmo, located on the northern rim of the Mesopotamian plains, and Jericho, in southern Palestine. According to scholar Norman B. Hunt, today Qalat Jarmo

has a series of archaeological levels contained within a 21-foot high artificial mound that show continuous occupation over a period of some 3,000 years. The village consisted of about 25 mud-brick multi-room houses built on stone foundations, together with storage pits for [wheat, barley, and other crops]. It is evident that the people of Jarmo had domesticated goats, sheep, and pigs, and probably also dogs and cattle.[4]

Onto the Plains

Over time, a number of small settlements like Qalat Jarmo grew larger, while new ones were built. Local population growth within the Fertile Crescent gradually increased until, by roughly 6000 to 5000 B.C., expansion onto the Tigris and Euphrates plains began. The next several centuries witnessed a slow but steady settling of Mesopotamia. The villages established there at first resembled Qalat Jarmo, but some slowly expanded into towns with populations of a thousand people or more. Among these communities were Tepe Gawra and Choga Mami in northern Mesopotamia, and Ur, Eridu, Uruk, and Tell al-Ubaid in the south, near the Persian Gulf.

Modern scholars call the residents of these small, early Mesopotamian towns Ubaidians, after Tell al-Ubaid. (It is unknown what they called themselves.) And appropriately, the era of Mesopotamian history lasting from around 5000 to 3500 B.C. is called the Ubaidian period. Exactly who the Ubaidians were remains somewhat unclear. But most scholars think they were migrants from the Fertile Crescent who may or may not have intermarried with peoples from other nearby regions.

Whatever their exact origins, the Ubaidians continued to maintain a village culture throughout their tenure as caretakers of the plains. Each village or small town consisted of a group of crude houses made from hard-packed earth and/or reeds gathered from the rivers. Hunt adds that some of the houses were "separated by alleys, with areas of larger and more elaborate buildings containing storage pits and granaries. A new feature was a central earthen mound surmounted by a single-roomed building, which presumably served a ritual [religious]

Trade was part of the Ubaidian culture. Some examples of exchanged goods were figurines, bowls, cups, and other ceramic (pottery) items.

function. During successive rebuildings at periodic intervals, these so-called temples became more complex."[5]

Archaeological evidence also indicates that the Ubaidian towns engaged in trade. Among the goods exchanged were figurines, bowls, cups, and other ceramic (pottery) items, some of them highly decorated with hand-painted geometric patterns. The existence of such craftwork and trade shows that at least some members of society devoted most or all of their time to nonfarming activities. However, nothing else of a substantial nature is known about the Ubaidians' social structure or customs.

The Sumerian Problem

Considerably more is known about the next major civilization to occupy the Mesopotamian plains. Sometime during the last few centuries of the fourth millennium B.C. (probably between 3300 and 3100 B.C.), a people now called the Sumerians took control of the area. The term *Sumerian* comes from word *Sumer*, the later Babylonian name for southern Mesopotamia. The Sumerians themselves called the area Kengir, meaning "civilized land." This was a very fitting definition, for as noted scholar Karen R. Nemet-Nejat writes, "the Sumerians turned an agricultural community into

The Sumerians became a cultural melting pot in which most people shared certain social ideas and customs. Shown here is a mathematical tablet showing the conversion of fractions and a division table.

Writing on Clay Tablets

The following concise summary of how cuneiform tablets were created and used is provided by the University of Pennsylvania Museum of Archaeology and Anthropology.

[In ancient Sumer] clay tablets were the primary media for everyday written communication and were used extensively in schools. Tablets were routinely recycled and if permanence was called for, they could be baked hard in a kiln. Many of the tablets found by archaeologists were preserved because they were baked when attacking armies burned the building in which they were kept. Clay was an ideal writing material when paired with the reed stylus writing tool. The writer would make quick impressions in the soft clay using either the wedge or pointed end of the stylus. By adjusting the relative position of the tablet to the stylus, the writer could use a single tool to make a variety of impressions. While many wedge positions are possible, awkward ones quickly fell from use in favor of those that were quickest and easiest to make. Like sloppy handwriting, badly made cuneiform signs would be illegible or misunderstood.

University of Pennsylvania Museum of Archaeology and Anthropology, "About Cuneiform Writing." www.upenn.edu/museum/Games/cuneiform.html.

the first urban [city-based] civilization in the world."[6]

The identity and origins of the Sumerians remain unknown. These mysteries lie at the heart of what modern scholarship calls the "Sumerian problem." One theory that attempts to solve that problem holds that they were simply local Ubaidians who became advanced enough to build cities and invent writing. An opposing theory argues that the Sumerians were *not* native to Mesopotamia. Instead, they migrated into the region from the east, possibly from what is now India.

Strongly supporting the second argument is the fact that the Sumerian language was different from the ones originally spoken in Mesopotamia. In fact, as Nemet-Nejat points out, "Sumerian is not related to any language, living or dead."[7] Indeed, many prominent place names in the area, including Eridu, Uruk, and Ur, are not Sumerian. This suggests that said names were Ubaidian and that, after conquering the Ubaidians, the Sumerians retained the old names for the sake of convenience. Other words the Sumerians borrowed from the Ubaidians include those for *farmer, fisherman, herdsman, potter, metalworker, carpenter, leather worker, weaver, mason, basket maker, merchant, priest, plow, furrow, date,* and *palm.*

Whether the Sumerians were locals who overcame their neighbors or interlopers from outside of Mesopotamia, there is no doubt that Sumerian culture swiftly came to dominate the region. It is important, however, not to associate that culture with any specific racial or ethnic group. During the Sumerian period, lasting from around 3300 to roughly 2000 B.C., numerous groups and peoples entered the area. And they were rapidly assimilated into Sumerian society. Thus, the Sumerians, like many later Mesopotamian peoples, became a sort of cultural melting pot in which most people shared certain social and religious ideas and customs. One could compare the situation to that of the modern-day United States. People of various racial, ethnic, and national backgrounds living in U.S. cities share a common culture called American. Similarly, the diverse peoples who lived in southern Mesopotamia during the Sumerian period shared a common culture that we call Sumerian.

The Potential of Writing

Sumerian culture contributed two fundamental advances to the ongoing rise of human civilization. One was writing. By 3000 B.C. at the latest, a small number of literate persons in Uruk and several other Sumerian population centers were using a writing system now called cuneiform. The word comes from the Latin term *cuneus*, meaning "wedge-shaped." Cuneiform consists of several hundred wedge-shaped marks that people made on moist clay tablets. When the tablets dried and hardened, they became the world's first versions of account sheets, letters, and books.

Later Mesopotamian peoples, including the Babylonians, Assyrians, and Elamites, adapted cuneiform to their own languages. Even after the Sumerians disappeared and Sumerian was no longer spoken, Sumerian cuneiform remained in use by scholars for several more centuries. But whatever the language, writing affected society in profound ways. People could now keep detailed financial records and inventories of goods. And by sending tablets by messenger, they could communicate over great distances without meeting face-to-face. Law codes, medical cures, and astronomical data could also be recorded in writing.

Yet though revolutionary, these uses only scratched the surface of the potential of writing. In time, the Sumerians began to produce written literature. Some of it was in the form of poetry that preserved their religious beliefs, prayers, and myths for future generations. Perhaps the most popular example was the thirty-five-hundred-line story of Gilgamesh, a Sumerian king who supposedly tried but failed to find the secret of immortality. (The original Sumerian version of the tale is lost; modern translations are based on later Babylonian versions.) Among the shorter literary forms were proverbs, which provide glimpses into everyday life and thought: "The poor men are the silent men in Sumer"; "Pay heed to the word of your mother as though it were the word of a god."[8]

Rise of Cities and City-States

The other crucial Sumerian cultural advance was the creation of the first cities. The Ubaidians had built and long maintained villages and small towns. These consisted of a few dozen, or at most a few hundred, houses and sometimes a small, central, temple-like structure. In contrast, the Sumerians erected vast enclaves having thousands of homes inhabited by tens of thousands of people, along with shops for merchants, palaces for rulers, and large religious structures, all enclosed by towering defensive walls. In this way, as Stephen Bertman says, the agricultural revolution "gave way to the 'urban revolution,' in which engineering and architecture came to play a larger and larger role. Cities arose that guarded their wealth behind moats and gated walls, while within these walls—amid winding streets and huddled dwellings and shops—stood administrative centers and temples, the new institutions of an invention called civilization."[9]

Modern historians are unsure which of the Sumerian settlements was the first to achieve city status. One proposed possibility is Eridu, then located close to the shore of the Persian Gulf. Other scholars think that Uruk, situated not far northwest of Eridu, was the first actual urban center that had a large population. Eridu, they suggest, may have served as a ceremonial center for Uruk's inhabitants. Whichever theory is right, it is worth noting that the Sumerians themselves claimed that Eridu was the home of the first king and the first civilized arts and works. Only later, the

The Sumerians were responsible for the creation of the first cities. Art works, like this statue from the Palace of Sargon II, came about as a result of these first urban centers.

Woolley Excavates the Sumerians

Charles Leonard Woolley was a pioneering archaeologist who unearthed Sumerian cities and artifacts in the early twentieth century. In 1922, he led a joint expedition of the British Museum and the University of Pennsylvania to the site of the ancient Sumerian city of Ur. Over the course of the next twelve years, he and his colleagues excavated numerous ancient graves, including some tombs belonging to Sumerian royalty. Woolley also studied the huge ziggurat at Ur, which in the city's heyday had been used for religious purposes. When he returned to England in 1935, he received a knighthood from the queen and thereafter wrote many books, some of which are still available and remain valuable for serious researchers and buffs of Sumerian civilization. These works include *The Sumerians* (1928); *Ur of the Chaldees* (1938); and *Excavations at Ur* (1954).

In the early twentieth century, archaeologist Charles Woolley unearthed Sumerian cities and artifacts.

story went, did the original seat of kingship move to other Sumerian cities.

Those other cities included Ur, Kish, Lagash, Umma, Sippar, and Nippur, among others. These were not dependent units within a larger Sumerian nation. Rather, they were independent city-states, each of which viewed itself as a small nation. Typically, each consisted of a large, central, walled town, around which stretched many square miles of farmland dotted with small villages that owed their allegiance to the urban center. Trying to remain self-sufficient, the people of each city-state grew a wide variety of crops and built irrigation canals to make sure the fields were well watered. Overall, most of these city-states must have resembled Nippur. Archaeological evidence shows that in the early to mid-third millennium B.C. (ca. 2900–2500 B.C.), its urban center was surrounded by almost two hundred villages, mostly located along five large irrigation canals and about sixty smaller canals.

As for the urban centers themselves, most were likely similar in appearance to Uruk. (Now called Tell al-Warka, it lies in southern Iraq; in fact, the name *Iraq* may have derived from *Uruk*, or from its biblical name, *Erech*.) Excavations, which began in 1912 and continue today, have revealed that about a third of Uruk con-

tained private homes and shops; another third had gardens and other open lands administered by the government; and the last third had temples and the sacred lands surrounding them.

Early Wars for Dominance

Although these early Mesopotamian city-states were in many ways self-sufficient, they were not always content

Local armies arose with the creation of early Mesopotamian city-states. At times, the reigning king led the armies to try to seize lands and possessions from neighboring cities. This relief depicts the daily life of Ur-Nanshe, king of Lagash, and his family.

with whatever resources and possessions they had accumulated. Sometimes one state coveted and tried to seize lands and villages belonging to a neighbor. This led to trouble, of course, as well as created the need for raising local armies. Such an army was led by the reigning king, who typically claimed either a connection with or the blessings of one or more of the gods worshipped by all Sumerians.

Farmland, crops, houses, water rights, and other kinds of property were not all these kings and their soldiers fought over. As Samuel Kramer points out, over time, "what had started out as limited economic rivalries turned into bitter political struggles for power, prestige, and territory. And the more aggressive among the early cities resorted to warfare in order to achieve their ambitious goals."[10] By the mid-third millennium B.C., these wars for dominance occurred on a regular basis. In around 2600 B.C., for example, Uruk defeated Kish. Not long afterward, Kish also suffered defeat at the hands of the king of Ur and his forces. Around 2500 B.C., however, Kish rose again in prominence and power and regained its lost lands. Meanwhile, in that same era, Umma and Lagash repeatedly went to war with each other.

Luckily for these competing, often warring cities, their early conflicts were fairly local and limited in scope. They did not cause the destruction of the urban centers or the slaughter of their populations. And each city-state survived to fight another day. This small-scale approach to interstate rivalry and warfare was about to change, however. Early in the 2300s B.C., a young man named Sargon was born somewhere in north-central Mesopotamia. He was destined to usher in a new era in which all of Mesopotamia, and even many lands lying beyond it, would be consumed by human lust for power and territory. The world's first age of empire was at hand.

Chapter Two

RISE AND FALL OF THE EARLIEST EMPIRES

The early Mesopotamians did more than create the world's first urban centers, writing systems, and standing armies. Using the latter, they also forged the first empires. The earliest of these imperial states was that of the Akkadian ruler Sargon, known to posterity as Sargon the Great, who reigned from around 2340 to 2284 B.C. (*Akkadian* is a general term that historians use to describe the people of northern Mesopotamia before Assyria rose to power there in the second millennium B.C. Coexisting with the Sumerians during the 3000s B.C., the Akkadians were culturally similar to them, the principal difference being language.) Sargon and his successors overran not only the Sumerian city-states in southern Mesopotamia, but also all of northern Mesopotamia and parts of what are now southern Iran. Not long after the short-lived Akkadian Empire's fall, circa 2190 B.C., a second large empire arose in the area. This one, known as the Third Dynasty of Ur, or more simply Ur-III, was based in Sumer.

Like the Akkadian realm, Ur-III lasted for only a little more than a century. But even though the two empires enjoyed relatively brief existences, they established important precedents for the region's future. The numerous large empires that rose and fell in Mesopotamia and the Near East in the millennia that followed used many of the political, administrative, and economic ideas and institutions utilized by the Akkadian and Sumerian imperialists.

Somehow More than Human

One of the key political institutions these rulers exploited to great advantage was kingship. The concept of a king, or *lugal* (Sumerian for "great man"), having absolute power over a people was not

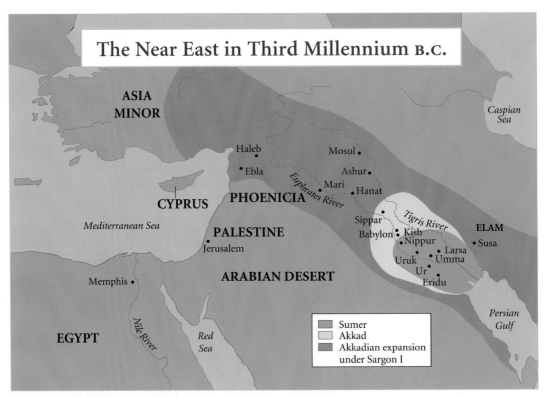

The Near East in Third Millennium B.C.

ASIA MINOR

Caspian Sea

Haleb

Mosul

• Ebla

Ashur •

CYPRUS   PHOENICIA

Mari

• Hanat

Euphrates River

ELAM

Mediterranean Sea

Sippar

Tigris River

Babylon • Kish

PALESTINE

Nippur

• Susa

Jerusalem

Larsa

Uruk   Umma

ARABIAN DESERT

Ur •

Eridu

Persian Gulf

Memphis •

EGYPT

Nile River

Red Sea

Sumer
Akkad
Akkadian expansion under Sargon I

This map shows early Mesopotamia in the third millennium.

new when Sargon rose to prominence. Kings had existed in Mesopotamia at least since the time of the expansion of towns into cities. According to Stephen Bertman:

> The office of *lugal* seems to have emerged at about the same time as Sumerian cities began to construct defensive walls to protect them from their enemies, and thus needed leaders in time of special emergency. . . . If the crisis persisted or repeated crises occurred, the *lugal*'s supreme authority may have become permanent, especially if . . . he relished

power and exercised it with verve [energy].[11]

To further justify assuming such permanent power, these early kings claimed that their right to rule had been given to them by the gods. This idea was reinforced by the high priests of local temples. They conducted ceremonies to reaffirm the king's divine connection and oversaw the creation of poetry and songs to celebrate it. Over time, therefore, the perception grew that the Mesopotamian kings, though not gods themselves, were somehow more than human. Some ancient texts mention an aura or radiance surrounding the king's person—the *melammu*, or "awe-inspiring luminosity." Also, high priests and high government officials commonly called the king the "son" of a certain god. And sculptures and paintings depicted the king standing beside one or more divine beings.

Superhuman or not, no monarch was capable of handling all the administrative, military, and religious duties of the government by himself. So Mesopotamian

Delegation was necessary for Mesopotamian monarchs. They used personal advisers and government ministers to oversee day-to-day matters such as building construction, irrigation projects, dispensing justice, and various economic matters. Shown here is a bronze hammer that was used around 2060 B.C., possibly in building construction.

Substitute Kings

The Sumerians and Akkadians, and later the Babylonians, Assyrians, and some other Mesopotamian peoples, practiced a distinct custom relating to the royal post of king. This was the selection of a so-called substitute king. This occurred in situations in which the safety of the monarch seemed at risk in some way, including bad omens (predictions of doom made by priests). The stand-in king had no actual authority. Palace officials dressed him in royal clothes and installed him in a comfortable suite of rooms inside the palace. Meanwhile, the real king went into hiding. If the perceived threat proved lethal, therefore, the substitute, rather than the genuine ruler, would die. "Once the danger was passed," scholar Stephen Bertman writes, "the substitute 'went to his fate'—an expression that implied death. In this way, the Mesopotamians hoped to trick fate. Becoming substitute king was not exactly a career move unless you were dying to sit on the throne."

Stephen Bertman, *Handbook to Life in Ancient Mesopotamia.* New York: Facts On File, 2003, p. 67.

monarchs learned to delegate much or even most of these duties to various governmental and religious officials. For example, high priests guided a king through his complex religious duties, which included leading public worship on holy days. And the king appointed generals and other military officers to run the army. Still, the king usually led the army on military campaigns. Mesopotamian kings also had personal advisers as well as government ministers to oversee such matters as building construction, irrigation projects, dispensing justice, and various economic matters.

The Akkadian Dynasty

Sargon and the other early Mesopotamian empire builders made these same sorts of royal appointments. But they needed larger numbers of high-ranking assistants. This is because their realms were far larger, more populated, more diverse, and therefore more difficult to oversee and rule than any yet seen.

Very little is known about how Sargon actually managed his vast empire. But modern scholars have been able to piece together a general picture of how he rose to power and created that realm. Born and raised somewhere in northern Mesopotamia, as a young man Sargon traveled to the Sumerian city of Kish. There, he became prominent among the advisers and officials serving that city's king. Eventually, Sargon was appointed to the post of military general. Soon afterward he defeated Lugalzagesi, king of the Sumerian city of Umma, who had been trying to subdue his neighbors, including Kish.

For reasons that are unclear, Sargon then struck out on his own and established a new city, Akkad (or Agade). Its location remains unknown. But it was likely not far from the city of Babylon, located some 60 miles (96.5km) south of the modern-day Iraqi capital of Baghdad. Now it was Sargon's turn to attack his neighbors. He seized control of Kish and then defeated all of the Sumerian city-states lying southeast of Babylon.

Sargon conquered many cities during his reign as the first member of the Akkadian dynasty.

More Akkadian conquests ensued, either under Sargon or one of his successors in the Akkadian dynasty (family line of rulers) he had founded. These included his sons, Rimush and Manishtusu; Manishtusu's son, Naram-Sin; and Naram-Sin's own son, Shar-kali-sharri. The Akkadian rulers captured Elam in southwestern Iran and the powerful city-states of Mari on the upper Euphrates and Ebla in Syria.

These successes were due in large part to the quality of the Akkadian army, the first known permanent professional military force. In part, it featured a highly efficient battlefield formation that had been used in Mesopotamia for some time. It consisted of rows of infantrymen (foot soldiers) standing close together so that their shields and spears overlapped. These troops "would advance," one military historian writes, "and thrust their spears in unison to provide maximum impact on the enemy and, at the same time, maximum protection for each spearman."[12] The Akkadians also used the composite bow (a more complex and lethal version of the ordinary bow), which may have come into wide use in the region under their rule.

Ur's Brief Days of Glory

The Akkadian rulers no doubt used their formidable army not only to conquer diverse city-states, but also to intimidate them into remaining loyal to the empire. Another tactic designed to maintain control was to put trusted Akkadians in charge of some of the subject cities. Nevertheless, the empire did not last long compared to many of the imperial

Sargon's Miraculous Childhood

Several later Mesopotamian accounts of Sargon of Akkad's life portray him in legendary terms. Supposedly, for instance, he had some kind of miraculous birth. And as an abandoned infant, he survived after being placed in a basket that floated down a river. One account that supposedly quoted Sargon himself read in part: "My mother was a priestess; I did not know any father . . . . My mother conceived me and bore me in secret. She put me in a little box made of reeds, sealing its lid with pitch. She put me in the river. . . . The river carried me away and brought me to Akki the drawer of water. Akki the drawer of water adopted me and brought me up as his son." Whether or not there is any truth to this story, many scholars think it inspired the biblical tale of the baby Moses set adrift in an Egyptian river.

Quoted in Werner Keller, *The Bible as History.* New York: Morrow, 1981, p. 123.

King Ur-Nammu (right) receives the symbols of justice from the moon god Nanna. An ambitious military leader, Ur-Nammu quickly gained supremacy over rival Sumerian city-states.

realms that rose later in the region. One important factor in its fall was a political reality that was to become a curse of all human empires. This is the tendency of conquered peoples to rebel and try to gain their independence. Indeed, the Sumerians and other subject peoples launched rebellions on a regular basis. And over time, in the words of noted scholar Gwendolyn Leick, the Akkadian realm "shrank to a small territory around the capital, which [now] fulfilled its function [only] in name."[13]

Greatly weakened, Akkad became vulnerable to attack. In around 2190 B.C., the Guti, a warlike people from the Zagros Mountains (lying east of the plains), captured what was left of the Akkadian realm. Almost immediately, any Sumerian cities that had not already regained their independence did so. These cities viewed the Guti as uncouth foreign intruders. And by roughly 2120 B.C., a coalition of Sumerian states had defeated the hill folk.

Prominent among the rulers who triumphed over the Guti was the king of Ur—Ur-Nammu (reigned ca. 2113–2094 B.C.). An ambitious and talented military leader, he swiftly gained supremacy over rival Sumerian city-states. The result was the second Mesopotamian empire, Ur-III. Ur-Nammu was a gifted administrator, and as his new realm expanded, he set up outlying provinces run by appointed governors who did the bidding of the central administration. He also launched large-scale building programs, including work on religious structures, canals, and improvements in Ur's defensive walls. Ur-Nammu seems to have been a popular ruler, at least among the people of Ur. When he died, they honored him with a hymn, which reads in part: "The wise shepherd . . . does not give orders any more. . . . Ur-Nammu, he who was beloved by the troops, could not raise his neck any more. The wise one lay down; [and soon] silence descended. . . . He could no longer bring pleasure to his wife with his embrace; he could not bring up his sons on his knees."[14]

Under Ur-Nammu's successors, Ur-III expanded. Shulgi (ca. 2094–2047 B.C.), son of the empire's founder, seized parts of Elam in southwestern Iran. And Shulgi's own son, Amar-Sin (ca. 2046–2038 B.C.), captured large sections of northern Mesopotamia. Both rulers skillfully exploited Ur-Nammu's strong administrative apparatus. And they used a system of standardized weights and measures, thereby making trade and commerce more efficient across the empire.

Like the Akkadian Empire before it, however, Ur-III was destined for a brief existence. The Elamites rebelled, and the Semitic-speaking Amorites raided Mesopotamia from the northwest. During the reign of Amar-Sin's grandson, Ibbi-Sin (ca. 2026–2004 B.C.), Ur fell to the Elamites after a long siege. The remnants of the empire then collapsed, effectively ending the era of Sumerian political power in Mesopotamia.

Indeed, at the time Ur-III's fall was widely seen as an almost earth-shattering event, and it inspired a poem that became a permanent classic of the region's literature. Titled *Lamentation over the Destruction of Ur*, it includes these powerful lines:

Ur [has been] destroyed, and as its destiny decreed . . . its inhabitants [have been] killed. . . . The people mourn. . . . [The] city was a ruin. . . . The roads were piled with dead. In the wide streets, where feasting crowds once gathered, jumbled they lay. In all the streets and roadways bodies lay. In open fields that used to fill with dancers, the people lay in heaps. The country's blood now filled its holes, like metal in a mold. Bodies dissolved like butter left in the sun.[15]

The Underbelly of Empire

Although neither the Akkadian Empire nor Ur-III lasted very long, they were illustrative of how large kingdoms in ancient Mesopotamia sustained themselves, as well as met the needs of their subjects. Conquering one's neighbors in the short term was one thing. Maintaining the large-scale economy of a far-flung empire in the long term was quite another. Once in power, imperial rulers needed to devote considerable time and energy to what might be called the economic "underbelly" of empire. This included acquisition of essential natural resources for local industries, maintenance and expansion of local agriculture and foreign trade routes, and the collection of taxes to keep the government and its armies and administrative systems running. In fact, the larger and more diverse the empire, the more the need for efficient management of these economic areas.

Trade is a clear example. During the years of the Akkadian Empire and Ur-III, there was a serious need to import foreign raw materials and other goods into Mesopotamia. This was partly because that region had (and still has) few natural resources. For example, copper and tin, the metals mixed to make bronze, then used for a wide variety of everyday objects, were scarce in the Tigris-Euphrates valley. Mesopotamia also had few forests for wood products or large deposits of stone for building projects. On top of these deficiencies, the era of empires witnessed increases in population, because of the expansion of agriculture and waves of immigrants entering the region. Also, the desire of imperial rulers to show off their wealth and power led to many large-scale building projects. In addition, says Leick, "Costly public

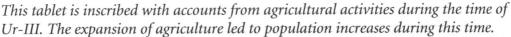

This tablet is inscribed with accounts from agricultural activities during the time of Ur-III. The expansion of agriculture led to population increases during this time.

festivals and displays of royal benevolence and respect [for] religion were regular features of the Ur kings' attempts to convince the population of their right to rule."[16] All of these factors increased the demand for imported raw materials and goods.

This administrative tablet from Ur-III is impressed with an official seal and lists plowmen and the wages they earned. Trade was regulated during this time and imperial administrators provided certain merchants with financial aid.

To help meet this demand, imperial administrators promoted and regulated trade. They sought out new, lucrative trade routes. And they provided selected merchants with financial aid, money that was used to build ships, warehouses, and roadside rest houses for the merchants. Moreover, as Leick points out, the Ur-III monarchs took their effort to maintain a sound economy a step further by imposing government control of key industries: "Production of textiles, one of the major Mesopotamian industries, was largely controlled by the palace, as was the import and export of various commodities and much of agricultural production."[17]

The rulers of the empires also increased the size and efficiency of tax collection. It is unknown exactly when taxation began in Mesopotamia. But evidence shows that both temples and central governments were already taxing local populations when the first major writing system appeared in the late fourth millennium B.C. Those who levied the taxes justified their right to do so partly on religious grounds. They reminded everyone that the land and soil, forests and marshes, and rivers and lakes had been created by the gods. Moreover, they claimed, these divinities trusted the kings and high priests to maintain the resources and permitted them to tax ordinary people for using these assets. This made taxation appear to be an inevitable part of the natural order.

Coins and paper money did not exist in the third millennium B.C., so taxes

Mesopotamia's Principal Weapon

Here, University of Calgary scholar Christon I. Archer describes the composite bow, the principal weapon wielded by Akkadian troops and other later Mesopotamian soldiers.

[The simple] or stave bow was in use at least by 3000 B.C. in Mesopotamia . . . but it was not until the development of the composite bow by the time of the Akkadian expansion [under] Sargon the Great and his successors, that the bow came to be the dominant weapon of the battlefield. . . . The composite bow was formed of wood, animal horns, animal tendons and sinews, and glue. As these substances were glued or bound together, and, before the string was attached, the bow was structured so that the two arms bent away from the body of the bow, thus creating great tension. The effective range of the bow was 250 to 300 yards.

Christon I. Archer et al., *World History of Warfare.* Lincoln: University of Nebraska Press, 2002, pp. 6–7.

Bow hunters in the forest, from a stone relief in the palace of Sargon. The composite bow was the principal weapon wielded by Akkadian troops and other later Mesopotamian soldiers.

typically took the form of goods and services. The average person paid the government or temple 10 percent of the crops and livestock he or she raised. Another way a person could pay taxes was to do a set amount of work on a state-sponsored construction project or to serve in the army for a certain length of time.

Keeping track of the amount of taxes each person owed and paid was difficult and time-consuming even in a single city-state. Because the early Mesopotamian empires were bigger and more populous than ordinary city-states, tax collection became an enormous job that kept hundreds or thousands of tax collectors busy year-round. The Ur-III rulers had a particularly complex system in which the central authority in Ur sent collectors to the outlying provinces. These men returned to the capital laden down with the taxes they had collected, including crops, livestock, furniture, pottery, and other craft goods. Government officials then stored, distributed, or traded these items as they saw fit. The workings of this system can be seen in the detailed records—on cuneiform tablets—that the imperial government kept, many of which have survived.

For Ur-III, all tax collection and other economic and political activities ceased, of course, after the empire's fall, circa 2004 B.C. The former subject cities were once more independent. Yet soon they would find themselves under the sway of new imperial masters. The rise and fall of empires was destined to continue, as control of Mesopotamia passed from the Sumerians and Akkadians to the Babylonians, Assyrians, and others.

Chapter Three

BABYLONIA, ASSYRIA, AND THEIR RIVALS

In the roughly thousand years following the fall of the Third Dynasty of Ur in around 2004 B.C.—now referred to as the second millennium B.C.—a wide variety of peoples vied for power in Mesopotamia. Some were native to the Tigris-Euphrates plains, chief among them the Babylonians and Assyrians. The latter, like the Akkadians before them, were based in northern Mesopotamia. The earliest capital of Assyria was Ashur, named for the chief Assyrian god. Ashur was situated on the Tigris's west bank about 60 miles (96.5km) south of modern-day Mosul, Iraq.

Meanwhile, the Babylonians largely replaced the Sumerians as caretakers of southern Mesopotamia. The principal Babylonian city—eventually the largest urban center in all of Mesopotamia—was Babylon. It was located on the Euphrates River just west of the old Sumerian city of Kish. Established sometime in the mid-third millennium B.C., Babylon remained a fairly insignificant town until it rose to prominence during the second millennium's first four centuries—what modern scholars call the Old Babylonian period (ca. 2000–ca. 1595 B.C.). The city became not only large and imposing, but also wealthy and a renowned cultural center. As such, it became a prize coveted by rivals and conquerors, both native-born and foreign.

Among those foreign powers that vied for control of Mesopotamia and/or other parts of the Near East in the second millennium B.C. were the Hurrians, Kassites, Hittites, and Egyptians. It appears that the Hurrians originated in south-central Asia, somewhere west of the Caspian Sea. They founded a strong kingdom—Mitanni—in the region lying between the upper reaches of the Tigris and Euphrates rivers. The Kassites likely entered Mesopotamia from the east, and

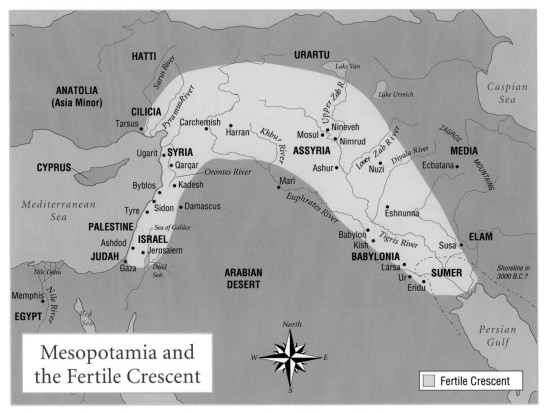

This map shows the region of Mesopotamia and the Fertile Crescent.

the Hittites hailed from the kingdom of Hatti, in central Anatolia. Finally, the Egyptians, whose homeland was centered on the Nile River in northeastern Africa, long played an important role in a sometimes dangerous rivalry among Assyria, Mitanni, and Hatti.

In the second millennium B.C., therefore, Mesopotamia and the regions that bordered it were frequently in a state of political flux. Large kingdoms and empires rose, fell, and/or struggled for supremacy. In this highly competitive situation, only the strongest armies, commanded by the most ambitious, clever, and relentless

kings and generals, could achieve even short-term success. "In the rapidly changing political climate," Gwendolyn Leick remarks, "the most tenacious leaders also needed particular character traits in order to stay in the game. They had to be quick-witted, decisive, patient, stubborn and charismatic, devious and ruthless. A tough physique and a talent for military strategy also helped."[18]

The Rise of Assyria

Among these larger-than-life leaders, the first to make a major mark for himself in the period following the fall of Ur-III was an Assyrian, Shamshi-Adad (reigned ca. 1813–1781 B.C.). In the years immediately preceding his birth, several large, independent city-states had risen to prominence in Mesopotamia. Isin and Larsa, for instance, enjoyed some success in the south, in the old Sumerian heartland. In the north, among the leading states were Mari, on the upper Euphrates, and Ashur, on the upper Tigris. Hailing from Ashur, Shamshi-Adad gained power there and cemented his prestige by erecting temples to the leading Assyrian god, Ashur, and the older Sumerian god, Enlil, who was still widely worshipped. "The temple of Enlil my lord," the king bragged in an inscription, "an awesome chapel, a mighty building . . . did I build in my city Ashur. To the temple I gave a roof of cedar-logs. In the chambers I set up doors of cedar wood with inlays of silver and gold . . . and I sprinkled the foundation with cedar oil, oil of the best kind, honey and butter."[19]

Shamshi-Adad's military endeavors were also impressive. He managed to seize Mari (about 140 miles, or 225 kilometers, southwest of Ashur) and to place his son, Iasmah-Adad, on that state's throne. This marked the beginning of the first of three periods of Assyrian expansion and empire in Mesopotamia. Not long afterward, Shamshi-Adad conquered Ekallatum, a populous city-state on the Tigris south of Ashur, and put another son, Ishme-Dagan,

The ancient city of Babylon, with its imposing size and great wealth, was the cultural center of Mesopotamia.

Honoring the Gods of Old

The Assyrian Shamshi-Adad erected a temple to the Sumerian god Enlil because Sumerian gods and religious customs survived in Mesopotamia long after the Sumerians themselves had disappeared. According to scholar Georges Roux:

For more than three-thousand years the religious ideas promoted by the Sumerians played an extraordinary part in the public and private life of the Mesopotamians, modeling their institutions, coloring their works of art and literature, pervading every form of activity from the highest functions of the kings to the day-to-day occupations of their subjects. . . . The fact that Sumerian society crystallized around temples . . . had deep and lasting consequences. In theory, for instance, the land never ceased to belong to the gods.

The most revered of the Sumerian gods were An, sovereign of the universe; Enlil, creator and ruler of Earth; Enki, god of the waters; and Enzu, Utu, and Inanna, deities of the moon, sun, and planet Venus, respectively.

Georges Roux, *Ancient Iraq*. New York: Penguin, 1993, pp. 90–91.

in charge there. In addition, the royal father pushed westward into what is now Lebanon, on the Mediterranean coast. Before returning to Assyria, Shamshi-Adad set up a *stele* (stone marker) that has survived. It reads: "My great name and my memorial stele I set up in the country of Laban [Lebanon], on the shore of the Great Sea."[20]

Meanwhile, the Assyrians were also active on the southern borders of their realm. Their chief rival there was Eshnunna, near the Diyala River (a major tributary of the Tigris). Shamshi-Adad did not attack Babylon (about 80 miles, or 129 kilometers, south of Eshnunna), however, perhaps because he deemed it too strong. Whatever his plans for subduing southern Mesopotamia may have been, his death in 1781 B.C. cut them short. At that point, Zimri-Lim, a member of Mari's original royal family who had fled during the Assyrian conquest years before, returned with an army. The rightful heir to that city's throne proceeded to depose Iasmah-Adad, a weak ruler, and take control.

Hammurabi Puts Babylon on the Map

Unlike Iasmah-Adad, Zimri-Lim was a skilled, vigorous ruler and diplomat. He made alliances with several city-states lying both north and south of Mari. He also expanded his city's trade volume; initiated large-scale building programs;

and carefully maintained Mari's large library of clay tablets bearing cuneiform writing.

What Mari's erstwhile, productive king did not foresee was that one of his new allies would turn on him. That double dealer was Babylon's ruler, King Hammurabi. The product of a line of Amorite kings who had established their dynasty in the city in around 1900 B.C. or somewhat later, he had ascended the throne circa 1792. Initially, Hammurabi pursued largely peaceful policies. He built irrigation canals, improved government administration, significantly expanded Babylon's size, and negotiated alliances

Babylon's ruler, King Hammurabi, pursued peaceful policies in the beginning of his reign, but then became ambitious and aggressive and became the first ruler in centuries to control all of Mesopotamia.

with Mari, Larsa, Eshnunna, and other neighboring states.

For reasons unknown, however, Hammurabi suddenly became ambitious and aggressive. Like Sargon and Ur-Nammu centuries before, he dreamed of conquering all of Mesopotamia. And to that end, in the late 1760s B.C., he began capturing neighboring states. Larsa, then the strongest state in southern Mesopotamia, fell to Hammurabi, as did Eshnunna and Mari to the north and northwest. He also overran Ashur and other major Assyrian cities on the upper Tigris. By the mid-1750s B.C., Hammurabi had put Babylon firmly on the map and become the first ruler in centuries to control all of Mesopotamia.

However, Hammurabi's huge imperial state turned out to be even more short-lived than Ur-III had been. He died in 1750 B.C. And his far less vigorous and talented successors were unable to hold the realm together. As Leick puts it, "One by one, the subject regions asserted their independence."[21] Nevertheless, Hammurabi and the first Babylonian empire exerted a great deal of influence on later peoples in the region. Thereafter, for example, Babylon remained the most splendid, envied, and sought-after city in the Near East. "Hammurabi's reign left a lasting impression on future generations," Karen Nemet-Nejat writes. For that reason, he was "one of the major figures of Mesopotamian history. . . . He [made] Babylon the recognized [major] seat of kingship, a position that remained uncontested until the Greeks [took control of the region later]. Babylon even survived as a [premiere Mesopotamian] religious center until the first century A.D."[22]

Justice for Everyone

Another important contribution Hammurabi made to later generations of peoples in the Near East was his law code, the most famous and influential set of laws before those of the Greeks and Romans in the first millennium B.C. His was not the first such code created in Mesopotamia. The king of the Sumerian city of Lagash had introduced a list of laws in the 2300s B.C., dealing with burial fees, treatment of women and orphans, and taxation. And Ur-Nammu, founder of Ur-III, had issued some laws that dealt with crimes such as rape and assault, providing various monetary fines as punishments. Somewhat later, still another Sumerian, Lipit-Ishtar, king of Isin, introduced laws that regulated the common Mesopotamian institution of debt enslavement. It consisted of a person agreeing to temporarily become someone's slave in order to pay back a debt.

However, none of these earlier law codes were nearly as comprehensive and widely influential as the one Hammurabi issued. He had his scribes etch his laws onto an 8-foot (2.4m) black stone *stele*, which fortunately has survived. The 282 statutes on the *stele* cover a wide range of issues. These include adoption, marriage, medical malpractice, property rights, money transactions, wine selling, and the regulation of wages and trade. Also, quite a few of the laws deal with issues surrounding personal injury, such as: "If a son strikes his father, they shall cut off his hand. If a man destroys the eye of another man, they shall destroy his eye. If he break another man's bone, they shall break his bone. If he destroy the eye of a client or break the bone of a client, he shall pay one mina of silver."[23]

These examples demonstrate that many of Hammurabi's laws carried heavy penalties. In fact, kidnapping, receiving stolen goods, breaking and entering, and even performing poorly in a government job could all result in execution. Yet there might be exceptions, depending on the social status of the accused. This is because Hammurabi's law code made distinctions for the wealth and status of the accused. Members of three general social classes—nobles and big landowners (*amelu*), ordinary citizens (*muskinu*), and slaves (*ardu*)—often received different sentences for the same offense. For example, wealthy people got stiffer

A section of Hammurabi's code. The laws inscribed on this stele *discuss issues such as marriage, property rights, and the regulation of wages and trade.*

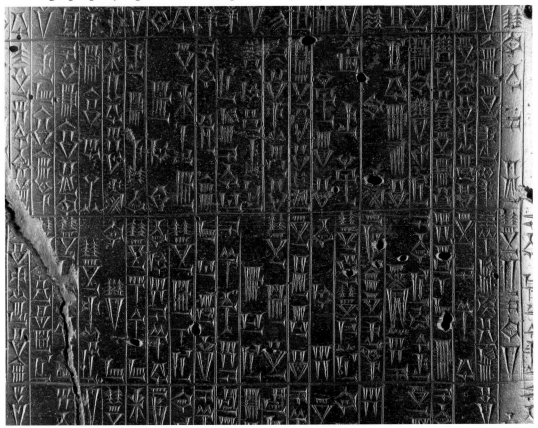

Hammurabi Speaks

The epilogue of the text carved on Hammurabi's famous stele *contains the following rationale, presumably in his own words, for creating his laws:*

The great gods called me, and I am the guardian shepherd whose scepter is just. . . . In order that the strong might not oppress the weak, that justice be given to the orphan and the widow . . . for the pronouncement of judgments in the land . . . and to give justice to the oppressed, my weighty words I have written upon my monument. . . . Let any oppressed man, who has a cause, come before my image [*stele*] as king of justice! Let him read the inscription on my monument! Let him give heed to my weighty words! And may my monument enlighten him as to his cause and may he understand his case! May he set his heart at ease! . . . In the days that are yet to come, for all future time, may [kings] observe the words of justice which I have written on my monument!

Quoted in Robert F. Harper, *The Code of Hammurabi.* Chicago: University of Chicago Press, 2007, p. 101.

Hammurabi's famous stele *includes an epilogue stated in his own words.*

punishments, probably because they were expected to act more honestly and honorably than lower-class individuals. Thus, Hammurabi's code was the first known set of laws that sought to ensure justice for everyone in society.

Kassite Babylonia and Mitanni

In the centuries following Hammurabi's death, Babylon, which had long been ruled by Amorites, came under the sway of two major foreign invaders. The first of these were the Hittites. Around 1595 B.C., led by their king, Mursilis I, they marched out of Anatolia, speedily crossed over northern Mesopotamia, and captured Babylon. Evidence suggests that the invaders received help from the Kassites, a crude hill people who had entered the region about a century before.

The Hittites barely took the time to celebrate their victory, however. It remains unclear why, but shortly after seizing Babylon they left and returned to Hatti. It is possible that Mursilis felt he had too few troops with which to enforce his rule on such a populous state lying so far from his homeland. In any

This stone lion was carved by Hittite sculptors. Shortly after capturing Babylon, the Hittites left Mesopotamia and returned home.

case, the departure of the Hittites left the Kassites in charge of Babylon and nearby sectors of southern Mesopotamia. Though culturally backward, the Kassites swiftly absorbed the local culture. As happened with numerous other Mesopotamian peoples over the centuries, they became "Babylonianized" in dress, language, and religious customs. (Their dynasty lasted from ca. 1595 to ca. 1155 B.C.)

The Hittites' departure had another unforeseen consequence. It created a momentary power vacuum in the region that allowed another outside group, the Hurrians, to gain a strong foothold there. Sometime in the 1500s B.C., they established a kingdom in the rolling hills lying west of Assyria. Not much is known about that once powerful ancient state, known as Mitanni. In fact, the location of its capital—Wassukanni—is still a mystery. Likewise, little is known about Mitanni's people and their customs. It appears that they had a wealthy ruling class that raised horses and developed a fearsome chariot corps. Clearly, the Mitannians needed a strong army, as they increasingly found themselves hemmed in by powerful enemies. Hatti lay to the north, Kassite Babylonia to the southeast, and Egyptian-controlled Syria-Palestine to the south.

Assyria's Second Empire

Directly along Mitanni's eastern side, a fourth enemy soon materialized. Following Hammurabi's absorption of Ashur and nearby towns two centuries before, Assyria had fallen largely into obscurity. But the locals had stubbornly refused to give up their traditional culture. And under a tough, ambitious ruler, Ashur-uballit I (reigned ca. 1365–1330 B.C.), they launched a new wave of conquests. Seeing that Mitanni's own leaders were engaged in a civil war, Ashur-uballit and his immediate successors crossed the border and seized large portions of Mitanni. Eventually, the Hurrian kingdom was completely absorbed, becoming the Assyrian province of Hanigalbat.

The offensives against Mitanni occurred along one of three major military fronts on which Assyria's aggressive kings operated. Also on that front lying west of the Assyrian heartland, they launched numerous attacks on Syria. These conquests had a ripple effect, as they threatened the stability of several small kingdoms in nearby Palestine, including the early Jewish states of Israel and Judah. The second major Assyrian military front stretched through the hilly regions along Assyria's northern border. Frequent raids into these hills netted the masters of Ashur large, valuable quantities of human captives, who became slaves, as well as horses, crops, metal artifacts, and other loot.

The third Assyrian military front was the border with Babylonia in the southeast. After several political disagreements and minor military campaigns, the Assyrian king Tukulti-Ninurta I (ca. 1244–1208 B.C.) captured Babylon.

This base, from the Ishtar Temple in Ashur, depicts King Tukulti-Ninurta I around 1220 B.C.

There, he erected a large new palace. He also celebrated his victory by commissioning the *Tikulti-Ninurta Epic*, the only example of Assyrian epic poetry that has survived.

The most accomplished of Tukulti-Ninurta's immediate successors was Tiglathpileser I (ca. 1115–1077 B.C.), who enlarged the empire on all three of its traditional military fronts. After Tiglathpileser's sudden assassination, however, Assyria's fortunes rapidly began to fade. His successors were far weaker and less effective rulers who were unable to stop various subject peoples from breaking away. And in only a few turbulent decades, the empire contracted until all that was left was the traditional Assyrian heartland centered around Ashur.

Conquest in God's Name

Assyria's King Tiglathpileser, who ruled from around 1115 to 1077 B.C., made the empire bigger than it had ever been. In his view, this feat fulfilled his duty to the god Ashur, namely to conquer in that deity's name. One of the king's inscriptions reads:

Ashur and the great gods, who have made my kingdom great, and who have bestowed might and power as a gift, commanded that I should extend the boundary of their land, and they entrusted to my hand their mighty weapons, the storm of battle. Lands, mountains, cities, and princes, the enemies of Ashur, I have brought under my sway, and have subdued their territories. . . . Unto Assyria I added land, unto her peoples, peoples. I enlarged the frontier of my land, and all their lands I brought under my sway.

Quoted in Daniel D. Luckenbill, ed., *Ancient Records of Assyria and Babylonia*. Vol. 1. New York: Greenwood, 1989, pp. 73–74.

The next century and a half proved to be a political and cultural dark age for the Assyrians. Indeed, their civilization seemed on the very brink of extinction. But they were a tough, proud, and resilient people. Soon they would rise again, stronger and bolder than before, and create a legacy of military prowess and imperial splendor matched by few other peoples in history.

Chapter Four

A Ruthless Spirit: The Neo-Assyrians

"Neo-Assyrian Empire" is the term modern scholars use to refer to the third, final, and greatest of Assyria's periods of expansion and empire, in the early first millennium B.C. At its height, in the seventh century B.C., the Assyrian realm stretched from southern Iran, westward across the Mesopotamian plains and beyond them to the Mediterranean coast; northward into Armenia (then called Urartu) and southeastern Anatolia; and southward into Syria-Palestine and Egypt. It was not only the largest empire yet produced by a Mesopotamian people, it was also the first empire that incorporated nearly the entire Near East.

Because of its great size and the number and diversity of its peoples, the Neo-Assyrian Empire was at all times extremely difficult to hold together and govern. One solution its leaders came to use was the creation of a system of provinces. "Governing each province," Samuel Kramer writes, "was a strong and efficient administration composed of Assyrian officials directly responsible to the king."[24] These governors kept local law and order, maintained roads and public buildings, and collected taxes.

Yet competent organization and administration were, by themselves, ultimately not enough to keep this great political-territorial giant intact. To ensure that conquered peoples stayed in line, Assyrian leaders resorted to torture, terror, and murder on a scale never witnessed before. Historian Chester G. Starr calls it a "parade of brutality and violence" that was openly, even proudly, depicted in Assyrian sculptures and other art. Starr notes: "The heads of conquered kings hung in the trees of the royal gardens. . . . Often the leaders in an area which rebelled were [slaughtered] by the hundreds and their grinning skulls piled

Assyrian leaders resorted to torture and murder on an unprecedented scale. This relief shows Assyrian warriors impaling Jewish prisoners on long spears after capturing the Jewish town of Lachish in 701 B.C.

neatly by the roadsides"[25] as a warming to other would-be trouble-makers.

Why did the Assyrian monarchs employ such unusually cruel methods? Most historians believe it was not simply that they were savage, barbaric individu-als. Rather, they viewed these methods as a practical means to their ends. On the one hand, they felt a duty to defend, protect, and perpetuate the Assyrian national identity and people, which had almost lapsed into oblivion in the recent past.

The Assyrian kings also felt that they had been assigned a historic, divinely inspired task. This was the subjugation of the known world under one central ruler, namely he who sat on the Assyrian throne. Importantly, the Assyrian kings believed that this mission was the will of their god, Ashur. They recognized "a religious, almost a moral motive," noted scholar Georges Roux points out. "The king's enemies were the god's enemies; they were 'wicked devils deserving punishment.'"[26]

Considering these factors, Starr suggests, the "ruthless spirit" of the neo-Assyrian monarchs was necessary "to break and harness the Near East." Because for the first time most of that region became united under one ruler, according to Starr, "the Assyrian period was in reality one of the greatest turning points in the civilized history of the area, and in this fact must be sought the justification for the booty and [brutality] of empire—if empire needs justification."[27]

Assyria Ascendant

This great turning point in Near Eastern history did not happen all at once. It was instead a slow but steady process that began in the late 900s B.C. as the Assyrians emerged from their dark age. At that time, Assyria consisted of a tiny expanse of territory measuring little more than 100 miles (160km) long and 50 miles (80km) wide, centered roughly where the Tigris and Upper Zab rivers

met. Most Mesopotamian peoples of that era likely viewed this region as a political and cultural backwash. Surely, they thought, it was destined never again to produce the kind of vigorous, successful leaders it had in past ages.

Yet this assessment proved shortsighted. It failed to take into account the pride, stubbornness, and resiliency of the Assyrian people and the toughness and boldness of their leaders. Starting with Ashurdan II (reigned ca. 934–912 B.C.) and his

Considered a great ruler, Emperor Ashurnasirpal II's realm covered all of northern Mesopotamia.

son, Adad-nirari II (ca. 911–891 B.C.), a succession of strong, talented kings began to lift Assyria out of obscurity. Ashurdan worked on rebuilding trade routes and the local economy. Later, employing a mix of military strength, terror, and intimidation, Adad-nirari recovered some of Assyria's lost cities in the plains west of the Tigris. His forceful approach set a precedent that nearly all later Assyrian rulers followed. They also copied the bombastic style of royal propaganda he established, as shown in one of his inscriptions: "Powerful in battle, who overthrows cities, who burns the mountains of the lands, am I. Strong hero, who consumes his enemies, who burns up the wicked and the evil am I. . . . Like the onset of a storm, I press on. Like an evil downpour, I rage. . . . At the mention of my mighty name, the princes of the [world's great nations] trembled."[28]

Adad-nirari's royal successors each tried to glorify himself, the nation, and the god Ashur through a combination of military conquests and the construction of temples, palaces, and other large public buildings. The conquests added more territory to the realm bit by bit during each royal reign. Many of the captured lands became new provinces in an empire that steadily grew at the expense of neighboring peoples. During the reign of the first neo-Assyrian king whom history came to see as a great ruler—Ashurnasirpal II (ca. 883–859 B.C.)—the realm covered all of northern Mesopotamia. That ruler also subdued most of Syria and reached the Mediterranean Sea. "In the Great Sea I washed my

Jehu, king of Israel, bows before King Shalmaneser III of Assyria. Shalmaneser III brought numerous new lands into the Assyrian realm.

Piles of Corpses

The cruelty and terror tactics employed by the Assyrian conquerors is well documented in their own records, including this excerpt from the chronicles of King Ashurnasirpal.

I captured the city. Six hundred of their warriors I put to the sword; 3,000 captives I burned with fire; I did not leave a single one among them alive to serve as a hostage. Hulai, their governor, I captured alive. Their corpses I formed into pillars [piles]; their young men and maidens I burned in the fire. Hulai . . . I flayed [skinned]. His skin I spread upon the wall of the city [and] the city I destroyed.

Quoted in Daniel D. Luckenbill, ed., *Ancient Records of Assyria and Babylonia.* Vol. 1. New York: Greenwood, 1989, p. 146.

weapons," he bragged. "I made offerings unto the gods and I fashioned a memorial stele [celebrating] my valor."[29]

The Imperial Army

The instrument of these frequent military ventures and strong-arm tactics was of course the imperial army. In the first century or so of the new realm, most of the soldiers were native Assyrians who were drafted, served on a campaign, and then returned to their farming or other professions. But in time many of these part-timers became professionals, making up a full-time standing army. Also, as the empire expanded, absorbing foreign regions, men from these areas were drafted to fill the ranks of the army's auxiliary units. (These foreign-born troops wielded whatever weapons were customarily used in their homelands.)

Part of why the army was so effective is that it was very well organized. At the top of the chain of command was the king, who usually personally led major campaigns and decided on basic strategy. His chief assistant, the *tartanu*, or field marshal, saw to the many details of the army's organization and field operations. The officers who ranked beneath the *tartanu* led units of 1,000, 200, 100, 50, and 10 infantrymen each. There were also commanders of the chariot units, each of whom commanded 50 chariot warriors and drivers.

The weapons these various kinds of troops wielded were little different from those used by the Assyrians and other Mesopotamians during the late second millennium B.C. The composite bow was still the chief offensive weapon. In a standard two-man field unit—the "archer pair"—one man held up a broad shield to protect the pair against incoming arrows and other missiles. The other man operated the bow, firing off one arrow after another. In a battle, rows of hundreds or thousands of these pairs moved forward in unison. Meanwhile, when possible, hundreds of chariots, each with a driver and archer, charged at the enemy. (Increasingly, the chariots were supplemented or replaced by cavalry—horsemen who could operate in hilly terrain in which chariots were impractical.)

Such a large, well-organized, and well-equipped army was highly effective, even devastating, on battlefields in that era. The fact is that the majority of Near Eastern kingdoms and city-states were small and lacked the resources to field armies of that size and caliber. It is no wonder, then, that Assyria's military machine continued to conquer new territories and to crush revolts by peoples whom the empire had already absorbed. For example, Ashurnasirpal's son, Shalmaneser III (ca. 858–824 B.C.), was victorious on all three of the nation's traditional fronts. He led his troops across Babylonia to the Persian Gulf in the south, into the Zagros Mountains in the northeast, and into Palestine in the southwest. One of Shalmaneser's immediate successors, Tiglathpileser III (ca. 744–727 B.C.), attacked and annexed most of Syria and overran half of Israel. A memory of the latter event was preserved in the Hebrew Old Testament: "In the days of Pekah, king of Israel, came Tiglathpileser king of Assyria, and took . . . Galilee [and] all the land of Naphtali, and carried [many] captive[s] to Assyria."[30]

Rise of the Sargonids

Although Tiglathpileser's conquests were impressive, they paled in comparison to those of the members of the greatest neo-Assyrian imperial dynasty. It was founded by Sargon II (ca. 722–705 B.C.), who was succeeded by his son, Sennacherib, grandson, Esarhaddon, and great-grandson, Ashurbanipal. Modern scholars call them the Sargonids (who should not be confused with the Akkadian Sargonids of the third millennium B.C.). Under them, the Assyrian realm reached its greatest extent.

Like all of his immediate predecessors, Sargon conducted military campaigns on a regular, almost yearly basis. The traditional war season was late summer (after harvest time in July) and early autumn. At other times of the year, the king involved himself in administrative duties and especially large-scale construction projects. The most impressive of these endeavors was the creation of a new capital city—Dur-Sharrukin ("Sargon's fortress"), situated about 15 miles (24km) northeast of the important city of Nineveh, in northern Assyria. Dur-Sharrukin replaced the former capital of Kalhu, which itself had earlier replaced the original capital of Ashur; the latter remained a ceremonial center and the burial site of Assyrian kings.

Only a year or so after establishing his new capital, Sargon died and Sennacherib (ca. 704–681 B.C.) ascended the throne. The new king first dealt with a troublesome situation in Babylon. There, a Babylonian nobleman named

The Rough March to Urartu

In around 714 B.C., Sargon initiated his conquest of Urartu (Armenia), which had recently tried to break away from Assyrian control. His royal records provide a vivid description of the mountainous regions his soldiers had to pass through on their northward journey.

They were high mountains covered with all kinds of trees, whose surface was a jungle, whose passes were frightful, over whose area shadows stretch as in a cedar forest, the traveler of whose paths never sees the light of the sun [and] on whose sides gorges and precipices [sheer cliffs] yawn, to look at which with the eyes, inspires fear. Its road was too rough for chariots to mount, bad for horses, and too steep to march foot soldiers over. With [a] quick and keen understanding . . . I had my men carry mighty pickaxes [and] they shattered the side of the high mountain [thereby] making a good road.

Quoted in Daniel D. Luckenbill, ed., *Ancient Records of Assyria and Babylonia.* Vol. 2. New York: Greenwood, 1989, pp. 74–75.

Merodach-Baladan had seized the city, as well as persuaded some Palestinian city-states to rebel against Assyria. Sennacherib chased Merodach-Baladan away and recaptured Babylon, almost destroying it in the process. "I devastated, I burned with fire," one of his inscriptions reads. "Through the midst of that city I dug canals, I flooded its site with water."[31] The Assyrian monarch then attacked the rebels in Palestine and made them forfeit heavy tribute (payment to acknowledge submission). Sennacherib is also noted for enlarging Nineveh, which he made his capital, and erecting there an enormous and splendid royal residence, the so-called Palace Without Rival.

Unfortunately for Sennacherib, he did not enjoy his new palace for very long.

In 681 B.C., his own sons murdered him. And after a short power struggle, the youngest of their number, Esarhaddon (ca. 680–669 B.C.), became king. His first major act was to rebuild Babylon, a gigantic undertaking that continued throughout his reign. "I built [Babylon] anew," one of his inscriptions reads. "I enlarged [it], I raised [it] aloft, I made [it] magnificent."[32] This vast urban renewal project won Esarhaddon the gratitude of most Babylonians, an unexpected turn of events in the long history of hatred between the two peoples.

In contrast, most other Near Eastern peoples viewed Esarhaddon with the same level of contempt they had earlier Assyrian monarchs, and with good reason. When the Palestinian city-state of

Sidon rebelled against him, his soldiers immediately went into action. They killed the local ruler, utterly destroyed the city, and deported all of its surviving inhabitants to a remote section of Assyria. Other small states in Syria-Palestine got the message and behaved themselves for the remainder of his reign.

The Egyptians also came to hate and fear Esarhaddon. Egypt had once been a mighty nation but had grown weak and vulnerable in recent centuries. Taking advantage of this fact, Esarhaddon

This relief, from the Palace of Ashurbanipal, shows the king and his queen feasting following the defeat of the Elamites in 653 B.C.

invaded Egypt in 671 B.C. and in less than a month captured its capital, Memphis. But to his dismay, he found that the Egyptians were every bit as proud, tough, and resilient as the Assyrians themselves. Two years later they rebelled. And Esarhaddon was forced to lead his army southward once again.

Assyria's Sudden Collapse

The third Sargonid, Esarhaddon, never made it to Egypt, however. During the trip, he died unexpectedly, and his son, Ashurbanipal (ca. 668–627 B.C.), took charge of both the throne and the expedition. The new king defeated the Egyptian rebels, commemorating his victory with these words: "With the help of Ashur [and] the great gods . . . who advance[d] at my side, I defeated [their] army in a battle on the open plain."[33] Nevertheless, the stubborn Egyptians continued to stage rebellions against the Assyrian occupiers, which kept many of Ashurbanipal's troops occupied.

The Assyrian monarch also had to commit large numbers of soldiers to the unenviable task of defending himself against his own brother. That upstart sibling, with the tongue-twisting name Shamash-shum-ukin, had long been ruling the city of Babylon in fulfillment of the dying wish of their father, Esarhaddon. For reasons that are unclear, Shamash-shum-ukin now decided to challenge Ashurbanipal for the imperial throne. The civil war lasted three years and ended with Shamash-shum-

ukin's defeat and death. Ashurbanipal next unleashed his wrath on the Elamites, who had backed his brother's bid for power. The Assyrian army cut a terrible path of destruction through Elam's heartland, burning crops, burning and looting the cities, and butchering the inhabitants.

In an unexpected turn of events, however, a similar fate was now in store for the Assyrians themselves. The exact events leading up to Assyria's abrupt, catastrophic collapse remain unclear. This is partly because in 639 B.C., the same year Elam met its doom, Assyrian royal record keeping suddenly stopped. The last twelve years of Ashurbanipal's reign must be pieced together from scattered foreign sources.

These records suggest that Assyria was rapidly torn asunder by a deadly combination of invasions, rebellions, and civil strife. Apparently, Ashurbanipal died in 627 B.C., and his sons, Assur-etil-ilani and Sin-shar-ishkun, fought each other for the throne. Sin-shar-ishkun was the ultimate victor. But the civil war had badly weakened the country, leaving it open to attack. The Medes, who had built a formidable kingdom in the hills of northern Iran, swarmed westward onto the plains. There, they joined forces with the Babylonians, who launched a major rebellion against their Assyrian masters.

Cyaxares II, king of the Medes, besieged and captured Ashur. Then, in 612 B.C., his troops, aided by those of the Babylonian prince Nabopolassar, swarmed across the Assyrian heartland.

They sacked city after city, culminating in the biggest and most splendid of them all—Nineveh. News of the city's fall swiftly spread far and wide. In distant Palestine, the Hebrew prophet Nahum heard the testimony of eyewitnesses and recorded it for posterity, saying in part: "Desolation and ruin! Hearts faint and knees tremble, anguish is on all loins, all faces grow pale!"[34]

Reconstructed in the mid-twentieth century, Nergal Gate was one of many entrances into the walled city of Nineveh, which was sacked by the troops of Cyaxares II in 612 B.C.

Increased Use of Horse Archers

By the time of the Neo-Assyrian Empire's rise to power in the Near East, chariots were no longer as numerous or important on the battlefield as they had been centuries before. They had been largely replaced by cavalrymen, who often operated in two-man units, as explained by Vanderbilt University scholar Robert Drews.

The earliest representations of archers shooting from the backs of galloping horses are ninth-century B.C. Assyrian reliefs. [They show] the cavalry archers operating in pairs. One cavalryman holds the reins of both his own and his partner's horse, allowing the partner to use his hands for the bow and bow-string. The early cavalry teams thus parallel exactly the charioteer and chariot archer. The cavalry archer was undoubtedly less accurate than his counterpart on a chariot. . . . But in other respects the cavalry teams were surely superior. They were able, first of all, to operate in terrain too rough for wheeled vehicles. And their chances for flight, when things went wrong, were much better. . . . If a cavalryman's horse was killed or injured, [he] could immediately leap on the back of his partner's horse and so ride out of harm's way.

Robert Drews, *The End of the Bronze Age: Changes in Warfare and the Catastrophe ca. 1200 B.C.* Princeton: Princeton University Press, 1995, p. 165.

Ashurbanipal leads a hunt as he readies his shot, from a late Assyrian stone relief at the Palace of Ashurbanipal.

A few Assyrian nobles and their followers managed to escape and make a last stand somewhere on the upper Euphrates. But the Babylonian-Median attack continued. And by 610 B.C., the Assyrian political state no longer existed. For Assyria, the relentless wheel of fate and history had come full circle and proved the old adage that one reaps what one sows.[35] Few nations in the human saga have risen to such heights of wealth and power as the Neo-Assyrian Empire did, and few have fallen from those heights with such speed and utter finality.

Chapter Five

TRIUMPH AND TRAGEDY: THE PERSIAN EMPIRE

The neo-Assyrian realm's thunderous downfall left an enormous gap in the leadership of Mesopotamia and surrounding regions. The Babylonians and Medes, who had brought about that downfall, expected and tried to fill the gap. But at the time neither possessed the quality of leadership and vision to forge and maintain an empire inhabited by dozens of diverse peoples.

That impressive feat was accomplished by the talented rulers who founded and shaped the largest political state yet seen in the Near East or the world—the Persian Empire. In the century following Assyria's fall, they rose from near obscurity in the region north of the Persian Gulf. With amazing speed, they defeated the Medes and overran the Mesopotamian plains. Babylon became one of several Persian capitals and a launching point for conquests of many more peoples and city-states in far-flung regions.

What made the Persians different, and ultimately more influential than the Assyrians was a markedly wiser and more effective style of imperial rule. Assyria's kings had spent almost all their time conquering new territories and putting down rebellions. Their empire was perpetually unstable, in large part because they were merciless rulers who inspired fear and hatred among their non-Assyrian subjects.

In contrast, Persia's kings employed a more measured and humane approach. True, they were conquerors. And most of the later ones were corrupt rulers. Yet they usually allowed their widely culturally diverse subject peoples a certain measure of independence. As a result, large portions of the empire enjoyed long periods of peace and prosperity. "By guaranteeing peace and order to the dutifully submissive," scholar Tom Holland writes, the Persian monarchs gave

A Persian soldier (left), and a Median soldier. Early Persian rulers absorbed the Medes and were significantly influenced by them.

future rulers of Mesopotamia and surrounding regions a kind of blueprint for "a multi-ethnic, multi-cultural, world-spanning state. As such, the influence of their example on the grand sweep of history would be [to create a] political model [that] would inspire empire after empire, even into the Muslim era [that marked the beginning of Mesopotamia's medieval period]."[36]

Median Interlude

To give credit where it is due, the early Persian rulers who fashioned this successful imperial model were themselves significantly influenced by the first people they absorbed. These were the Medes, who arose in the hill country of western and northern Iran in around 1000 B.C. During the years in which the neo-Assyrian realm was spreading across the Near East, the Medes slowly grew more populous and ambitious. The two peoples did come to blows from time to time, as revealed in the inscriptions of the Assyrian monarchs Tiglathpileser III and Sargon II. But Media's remoteness and rocky terrain discouraged the Assyrians from launching a full-scale invasion, so the Medes escaped conquest.

In around 625 B.C., shortly after the outbreak of civil war in Assyria, Cyaxares II became king of Media. A talented and energetic ruler, he launched large-scale military reforms that made the Median army a force to be reckoned with. Many of his soldiers were native Medes. However, he also drafted numerous men from minor Iranian peoples who had come under Median control, including the Persians. According to the fifth-century-B.C. Greek historian Herodotus, Cyaxares had his archers, spearmen, and cavalry undergo separate and specialized training. "Previously," Herodotus wrote, these different kinds of fighters "had all been mixed up in a mob."[37] Cyaxares also introduced military uniforms that became standard not only for Median soldiers, but also later for Persian troops.

Each man wore a long-sleeved leather tunic that ended above the knee, leather trousers, laced shoes with projecting tips, and a round felt cap with a neck flap.

The new, improved army proved its worth during Cyaxares' bold attack on the Assyrian heartland in 614 B.C. After Assyria had been crushed, the Medes and their allies, the Babylonians, divided the conquered lands among themselves. And to reinforce the new alliance, Cyaxares married his daughter (or perhaps granddaughter), Amytis, to Nebuchadnezzar II, who had succeeded his father Nabopolassar as Babylonia's king. (It was for Amytis that Nebuchadnezzar erected the famous "Hanging Gardens of Babylon," later listed among the seven wonders of the ancient world.)

Cyaxares also launched new conquests intended to expand Median wealth, prestige, and power. Moving northeastward, he assaulted the peoples who dwelled in the forests along the southern shore of the Caspian Sea. Then he turned westward and overran Urartu, which had enjoyed a brief period of independence after Assyria's collapse. Later, in 585 B.C., he invaded Lydia, a powerful kingdom that then controlled central and western Anatolia. This expedition failed, however, and Cyaxares died that same year.

Cyrus the Great

Succeeding Cyaxares on Media's throne was his son, Astyages. Unlike his father, Astyages was a mediocre king. And under his largely weak rule some of his vassals

The Neo-Babylonian Empire

King Nabopolassar, whose alliance with the Median king Cyaxares sealed Assyria's fate, was the first ruler of what modern scholars often call the Neo-Babylonian dynasty and empire. It lasted less than a century—from 626 to 539 B.C. Yet its reputation and impact were considerable because its kings were wealthy and energetic builders who erected cities, temples, palaces, and bridges far and wide. Nabopolassar's son, Nebuchadnez-zar II (reigned 605 to 562 B.C.), built the most famous of all these monuments—the Hanging Gardens of Babylon (for his wife, a Median princess who missed the forests of her native land). The rulers who followed him on the throne included Amel-Marduk, Neriglissar, Labashi-Marduk, and Nabonidus. The latter was defeated by Persia's King Cyrus II in 539 B.C., bringing the Neo-Babylonian dynasty to an end.

An illustration of the reconstructed city of Babylon, shows the Hanging Gardens in the foreground and the Tower of Babel in the distance.

The mausoleum (burial chamber) of Cyrus the Great is located in Pasargadae, Iran. Cyrus was considered a skilled, dynamic, and inspirational ruler.

(conquered peoples within the Median Empire) considered trying to gain their independence. Outstanding among these peoples were the Persians, who hailed from Fars, on the northeastern shore of the Persian Gulf. "The Persians had long resented their subjection to the Medes," Herodotus said. "At last they had found a leader and welcomed with enthusiasm the prospect of liberty."[38]

That leader was Cyrus II (later called "the Great"), who at the age of about forty-one became the local ruler of Fars in 559 B.C. He launched a carefully planned revolt against the Medes in 553 and roughly three years later captured their capital of Ecba-tana, in the mountains directly east of central Mesopotamia. At that point, most of Astyages' remaining troops apparently felt that Cyrus would be a better king. And in Herodotus's words, in the moment of truth many of them "deserted to the Persians." Those who remained with Astyages "were killed and he himself was taken alive."[39]

Cyrus proved to be a skilled, dynamic, even inspirational ruler. Almost immediately, he displayed exceptional wisdom by letting Astyages and other high Median officials live and join the royal court. Cyrus also embraced and absorbed, rather than eradicated, Media's rich culture.

Similarly, he made Ecbatana his second capital (after Fars's chief city, Pasargadae) and ordained Media the first and leading satrapy, or province, of the new Persian Empire. (*Satrapy* was one of several words the Persians borrowed from the Medes.) These and other constructive acts showed Cyrus to be an effective, fair, and just ruler and won him the admiration of Persian subjects far and wide.

Though Cyrus was unarguably a benevolent king, he was also an ambitious imperialist who desired to expand the size of his realm. But to achieve this goal, he required a large, effective army. On the one hand, he took full advantage of the Median military reforms instituted by Cyaxares a few decades before. On the other hand, Cyrus borrowed several aspects of Assyrian military organization, modifying and improving that system in various ways. He increased the number of archer pairs on the battlefield, for example, which produced a thicker, more deadly rain of arrows. He also developed an elite unit of mounted fighters, all members of the Persian nobility. In addition, he made military service an obligation for all Persian men between the ages of twenty and twenty-four, although some stayed on well into their thirties or even forties.

With his new and improved military machine, Cyrus swiftly conquered one

A Persian Royal Procession

The royal court of the Persian Empire was famous for its wealth and splendid displays of magnificence. This account, by the fourth-century-B.C. Greek writer Xenophon, describes a royal procession in the era of Cyrus II (the late 500s B.C.).

When the palace gates were thrown open, there were led out at the head of the procession four abreast some exceptionally handsome bulls. . . . Next after the bulls came horses, a sacrifice for the Sun; and after them came a chariot. . . . It was drawn by white horses with a yoke of gold and wreathed with garlands.

. . . After that came [a] chariot with horses covered with purple trappings, and behind it followed men carrying fire on a great altar. Next after these Cyrus himself upon a chariot appeared. [He was] wearing his tiara [crown] upright, a purple tunic . . . trousers of scarlet dye about his legs, and a mantle all of purple. . . . When Cyrus's chariot had come forth, four thousand lancers took the lead [and] his mace-bearers, about three hundred in number, followed next in gala attire.

Xenophon, *Cyropaedia*, trans. Walter Miller. New York: Macmillan, 1914, vol. 2, pp. 355–357.

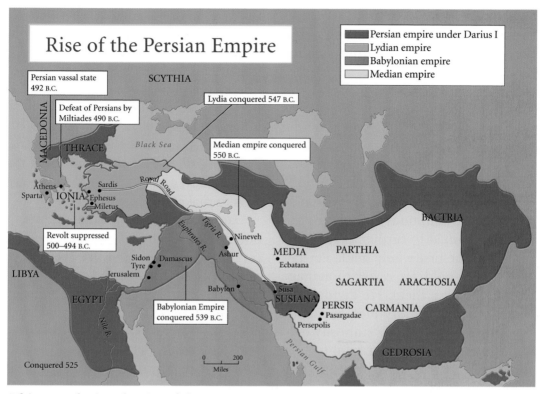

Rise of the Persian Empire

Legend:
- Persian empire under Darius I
- Lydian empire
- Babylonian empire
- Median empire

SCYTHIA

Persian vassal state 492 B.C.

Defeat of Persians by Miltiades 490 B.C.

Lydia conquered 547 B.C.

MACEDONIA

THRACE

Black Sea

Median empire conquered 550 B.C.

Athens • Sardis
Sparta • IONIA • Ephesus
Miletus

Royal Road

BACTRIA

Revolt suppressed 500–494 B.C.

Euphrates R.

Tigris R.

Nineveh •

MEDIA

PARTHIA

Sidon • Damascus
Tyre • Ashur •
Jerusalem •

Ecbatana •

LIBYA

Babylon •

Susa •

SAGARTIA

ARACHOSIA

EGYPT

Babylonian Empire conquered 539 B.C.

SUSIANA

PERSIS

CARMANIA

Pasargadae •

Nile R.

Persepolis •

Persian Gulf

GEDROSIA

Conquered 525

0   200
Miles

This map depicts the rise of the Persian Empire under Darius I.

Mesopotamian and Near Eastern region after another. Lydia fell to his troops in 547 B.C. and became a Persian satrapy. And in 539 B.C., he invaded Babylonia and defeated its king, Nabonidus. Entering Babylon in triumph, Cyrus proclaimed: "I am Cyrus, king of the universe, Great King, mighty king, king of Babylon, king of Sumer and Akkad, king of the world quarters."[40] Because Nabonidus's empire had included all of southern Mesopotamia and most of Palestine, these lands now became part of the Persian realm. Cyrus wanted to invade and annex Egypt next. However, he died in 530 B.C., leaving further expansion of the empire to his immediate successors.

Cambyses and Darius

The first of these rulers was Cyrus's son, Cambyses II. The new king ordered that preparations for the Egyptian invasion should continue. Importantly, they included the building of a fleet of warships, Persia's first, marking its growth from strictly a land power to a combined land and sea power. This made it potentially easier for Persia to launch campaigns into the Mediterranean region and into the lands lying east of the Persian Gulf.

The first test for the new navy came when Cambyses attacked Egypt in 525 B.C. The Persian ships sailed down the Palestinian coast, supporting the Persian land army as it marched southward. Cambyses defeated the pharaoh Psamtik III in the Nile Delta. And the rest of Egypt then rapidly fell to the invaders.

To consolidate his gains, Cambyses stayed in Egypt for three years. He was on his way home in 522 B.C. when he died, possibly of an infection acquired from a simple knife cut. His successor was a Persian nobleman who ascended the throne as King Darius I. Persia's new leader was as ambitious as his predecessors and wanted to further expand the realm. But he first wisely made Persia's already vast holdings easier to manage by reorganizing them. He divided the empire into twenty satrapies, giving the governor of each satrapy authority over local government but not local troops. The latter came under the command of specially appointed military generals who reported directly to Darius. The king next assigned standard annual tax rates to each province, ensuring a reliable flow of wealth into the royal treasury. Another effective economic reform was his introduction of coinage (an idea borrowed from the Lydians). Made of gold, Darius's coins were called *darics*, possibly after himself.

Darius also improved the realm's organization and efficiency by constructing a large-scale system of roads. These allowed royal messengers and armies, as well as merchants and traders, to move quickly from one part of the empire to another. The most famous of these roads, which had surfaces of hard-packed earth, stretched over 1,500 miles (2,414km)

from Susa, near the head of the Persian Gulf, to Sardis, near the shore of the Aegean Sea. Herodotus, who actually traveled on this highway, recalled: "At intervals all along the road are recognized stations, with excellent inns. . . . The total number of stations, or post-houses, on the road from Sardis to Susa is 111. . . . Traveling at the rate of 150 furlongs [18 miles] a day, a man will take just ninety days to make the journey."[41]

Darius's roads made it easier for him to pursue his new military ventures, which carried his armies far from the center of the Persian realm in southern Mesopotamia and Fars. In the east, Persian troops conquered the rugged region lying northwest of India in 519 B.C. Only a few years later, Darius turned his attention westward, to Scythia, the area lying west of the Black Sea (now occupied by Bulgaria and Romania). In 512 B.C., Darius crossed what is now the Bosporus Strait and marched northward into Scythia. This was the first time a Mesopotamian-based empire had invaded Europe.

It was not long, however, before Darius was forced to turn his attention farther southward. Years before, in conquering Lydia, Cyrus had incorporated into the Persian Empire a string of Greek cities lying along Anatolia's western coast, a region then called Ionia. In 499 B.C., the Ionian Greeks rebelled against their Persian overlords. Darius fairly easily crushed the insurrection. But he angrily noted that two city-states of mainland Greece—Athens and Eretria—had aided the Ionian rebels.

Bent on punishing what he saw as upstarts who had dared to interfere in his affairs, in 490 B.C. Darius sent an army commanded by two of his generals across the Aegean. They successfully sacked Eretria. But not long afterward, on the plain of Marathon, near Athens, the Athenians decisively defeated the invaders. This was by no means a major disaster for what had become the largest,

A staircase and columns at the Palace of Darius in Persepolis, Iran. Darius reorganized Persia's vast holdings to make them easier to manage.

strongest empire in the world. But it *was* a blow to the great king's prestige and ego. So he prepared to retaliate with a massive attack on Greece.

Persia's Decline and Fall

In 486 B.C., however, before he could enjoy his revenge, Darius died, and his son, Xerxes (*ZERK-seez*), ascended Persia's throne. The new king decided to carry out the projected Greek expedition. His forces, which moved into Greece in 480 B.C., consisted of about two hundred thousand land troops and almost a thousand ships (the largest invasion force assembled anywhere in the world in ancient times). But Xerxes was no

The Tomb of Xerxes I was built into the side of a mountain in Naksh-i-Rustam, Iran. Xerxes tried to invade Greece, but was unsuccessful.

Persian Army Organization

The Persian imperial army broke down into regiments of a thousand men each. According to Nick Sekunda, a noted scholar of ancient armies:

The Old Persian term for one of these regiments was *hazarabam*. [Each] was commanded by a *hazarapatis*, or "commander of a thousand," and was divided into ten *sataba* of a hundred. Each *satabam* [was] in turn divided into ten *dathaba* of ten men. The *dathabam* of ten formed the basic tactical sub-unit in the infantry, and was drawn up on the battlefield in file [one man behind another]. The *dathapatis* [commander of a *dathabam*] was stationed in the front rank. . . . Behind him the rest of the *dathabam* would be drawn up in nine ranks, each man armed with a bow and falchion [curved sword].

Persian units larger than a regiment also employed the decimal system. The Persian name for a unit made up of ten hazaraba, *or ten thousand men, is unknown. But the Greeks called it a "myriad." The leading myriad was the one manned by the king's elite personal bodyguard, the* Amrtaka, *or "Immortals."*

Quoted in John Hackett, ed., *Warfare in the Ancient World.* New York: Facts On File, 1990, pp. 83–84.

more successful against the Greeks than his father had been. In a series of now legendary battles, a few tiny but scrappy and freedom-loving Greek city-states inflicted enormous casualties on the Persians and drove them back into Anatolia.

Xerxes decided that mounting another huge invasion so far from Fars and Mesopotamia would be too costly and time-consuming. So he never attempted to enter Europe again (nor did any other Persian monarch). Moreover, lacking his father's vision and administrative skills, Xerxes fared no better in his domestic affairs. Most of the rest of Xerxes' reign was marred by court schemes and polit-

ical corruption, eventually inviting a coup by ambitious palace and military officials. In 465 B.C., they assassinated the king and installed his eighteen-year-old son, Artaxerxes, on the throne.

Unfortunately for Persia, Artaxerxes and most of his successors were even less effective rulers than Xerxes had been. They became heavily involved in personal pursuits and internal power struggles and lost interest in expanding the realm, as well as in improving conditions in the existing provinces. This caused increasing discontent among Persia's subject peoples, especially those situated far from the Persian heartland.

So over time, rebellions became more common. And when the last Persian king, Darius III, was crowned in 336 B.C., the empire, though still vast, was weak and vulnerable to outside attack. The great triumph of Persia's kings had been to create a mighty and stable centralized imperial state. Their ultimate tragedy had been to allow its complex, workable framework to weaken.

The reality of Persia's decline was not lost on the Greeks. Under the pretext that he was avenging Xerxes' invasion more than a century earlier, Philip II, king of the Greek kingdom of Macedonia, prepared to invade Persian-controlled Anatolia and Mesopotamia. Philip was unexpectedly assassinated, however. And it was his son, Alexander III (later called "the Great"), who would bring the Persian giant to its knees between 334 and 330 B.C. This would lay the groundwork for nearly two centuries of Greek rule in Mesopotamia.

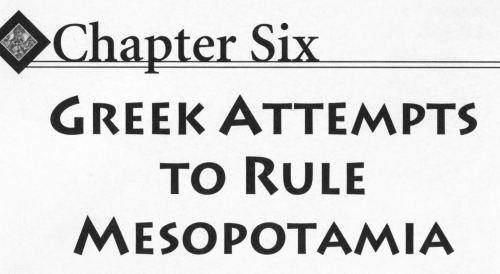

Chapter Six

GREEK ATTEMPTS TO RULE MESOPOTAMIA

The Greek dream of conquering the Persian Empire and seizing the rich Mesopotamian plains did not originate with Philip II and his ambitious son, Alexander. In fact, in 344 B.C., the noted Athenian orator Isocrates had called on Philip to unite the Greek states in a war on Persia. The Greeks had come to see the Persians as "effeminate [unmanly] and unversed in war and utterly degenerate from luxurious living," Isocrates said. Yet no Greeks had thus far "aspired so high as to attempt to make us masters of Persia." The Greeks "do not even have the spirit to pay them back for the injuries we have suffered at their hands,"[42] he added, referring to the Persian invasion of Greece in the previous century.

Isocrates had come to believe that a Greek conquest of Persia was quite doable in large part because of the exploits of the "Ten Thousand." In 401 B.C., when Isocrates was in his thirties, a young Persian nobleman, Cyrus the Younger, had attempted to seize the throne of his older brother, King Artaxerxes II. Among the troops Cyrus had gathered were ten thousand Greek mercenaries. At Cunaxa, near Babylon, Artaxerxes defeated and killed Cyrus. But the Greek troops emerged from the battle largely intact and, finding themselves stranded in enemy territory, these men fought their way out of Mesopotamia and made it back to their homes.

The Ten Thousand had confirmed what was already common knowledge in the Greek world. Namely, Greek infantrymen were superior in battle to Persian soldiers. More importantly, if such a small, ill-supplied Greek force could survive a trek through Persia's heartland, what havoc might a far larger and better supplied Greek army wreak on the Persians?

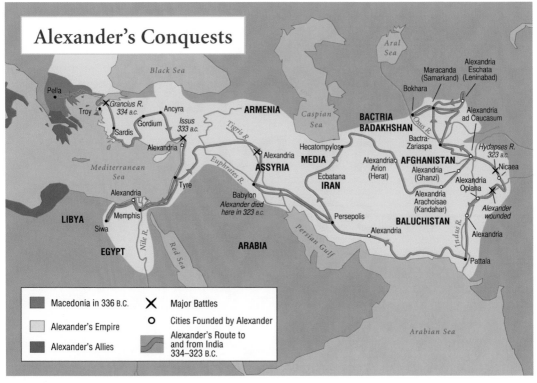

This map depicts the conquests of Alexander.

Alexander and the Successors

Thus, when Alexander led his father's army into Persia in 334 B.C., he and his troops were supremely confident of victory. These troops numbered about thirty-two thousand foot soldiers and five thousand cavalry. Persian forces were much larger but were unable to stop the invaders' nearly irresistible attack. Alexander defeated a Persian army at the Granicus River, in western Anatolia; routed another, larger force, this one led by King Darius III himself, at Issus, in Syria; then marched southward through Palestine and freed Egypt from Persian control.

Having secured Egypt, Alexander headed northeastward into Mesopotamia. There, at Gaugamela, near where the old Assyrian capital of Nineveh now lay buried by dirt and debris, Darius was waiting with an army of at least one hundred thousand soldiers. According to Alexander's later Greek biographer Arrian, the Macedonian king opened the battle by leading his right wing in an assault on the Persian left wing, which "collapsed the very moment he was on them." Not long afterward, "Alexander's victorious right wing, seeing the Persians opposite them already in flight, now swung left toward the center [and] forced them back. . . . [Soon] Darius himself was in flight. That was the signal for a general rout. . . . Thousands of panic-stricken [Persian troops] struggled in hopeless disorder to escape."[43]

After the enormous Greek victory, in which tens of thousands of Persians perished, Darius eluded Alexander for several months. It became increasingly clear to Darius's leading supporters that the empire could not recover. So they finally killed him, hoping to gain favor for themselves from Alexander. He responded by having their leader, Bessus, torn limb from limb for denying Alexander the privilege of dealing with his enemy in his own way.

Claiming Darius's empire as his own, Alexander made the respected old Mesopotamian city of Babylon his new capital. In fact, he planned for Babylon to become the center of a true world empire. He hoped it would eventually include India in the east and most of Europe in the west, in addition to the many lands he already controlled—Greece, Mesopotamia, Iran, Syria-Palestine, Egypt, and Anatolia. However, after more than five years of campaigning in the east, including India, Alexander returned to Babylon. And there he died, at age thirty-three (possibly of alcohol poisoning), in 323 B.C.

The forces of Alexander defeated the army of King Darius III at the site of this Roman aqueduct in 333 B.C.

Leaders Exchange Words

Following Alexander's defeat of King Darius III at Issus (in 333 B.C.), the two leaders exchanged letters. Darius said: "[Alexander] has crossed into Asia with his armed forces and done much damage to the Persians. For this reason [I] took the field in defense of [my] country and of [my] ancestral throne. . . . Now Darius the King asks Alexander the King to restore from captivity his wife, his mother, and his children [whom Alexander held as hostages]."

Alexander answered Darius:

Your ancestors invaded . . . Greece and caused havoc in our country, though we had done nothing to provoke them. As supreme commander of all Greece I invaded Asia because I wished to punish Persia for this act. . . . By God's help I am master of your country. . . . Come to me, therefore, as you would come to the lord of the continent of Asia. . . . And in the future let any communication you wish to make with me be addressed to the King of all Asia. Do not write to me as an equal [or] I shall take steps to deal with you as a criminal.

Quoted in Arrian, *Anabasis Alexandri*, published as *The Campaigns of Alexander,* trans. Aubrey de Sélincourt. New York: Penguin, 1986, pp. 126–128.

Although the conqueror of Persia was gone, the Greeks were in Mesopotamia and other parts of the Near East to stay. Thousands of Greek soldiers, farmers, administrators, merchants, craftsmen, and scholars migrated from Macedonia and the Greek city-states. They settled down to work and raise families in the same areas that the Sumerians, Assyrians, Babylonians, Elamites, and Medes had once called their homelands. These lands still had largely Persian populations, of course, and some of the Greek immigrants intermarried with Persian women.

Meanwhile, Alexander's leading generals and governors fought one another for control of his huge, though short-lived, realm. Known to posterity as the "Successors," they waged a series of bloody wars that lasted, off and on, for nearly two generations. One of the few Successors who emerged alive from these struggles was Ptolemy (*TAW-luh-mee*). He seized control of Egypt, which became the center of the Ptolemaic Empire (whose last ruler was the famous Queen Cleopatra VII). Another of Alexander's chief commanders, Seleucus, became the first ruler of the Seleucid Empire, named after its founder. It encompassed all of Mesopotamia and broad sections of southern Iran, Syria-Palestine, and Anatolia.

Seleucid Rule in Mesopotamia

Today, the Seleucid realm and other Greek political states that emerged in the Near East during and soon after the wars of the Successors are termed Hellenistic, meaning "Greek-like." (Its root is *Hellenes*, the word the ancient Greeks used to describe themselves; Greece itself was called Hellas.) This name reflects the fact that their societies often featured various Near Eastern languages, customs, and ideas overlaid by a thin surface of Greek ones. The phenomenon was particularly evident in Mesopotamia and other Seleucid-controlled territories. It produced a socially and economically classist society in which Greeks and a few wealthy Persians and other non-Greeks

This coin bears the likeness of Seleucus I, one of Alexander's chief commanders.

enjoyed higher status and more privileges than the bulk of the native population. Not surprisingly, fluency in Greek language and the practice of Greek customs became crucial to achieving success in urban areas, especially in government circles.

Yet Greek culture did not creep into the Mesopotamian countryside to an equal degree. As Norman Hunt puts it, there always remained "a division between Greek practices in the cities and Persian ones in the rural areas."[44] Indeed, most rural Mesopotamians continued to converse in traditional local languages, notably Aramaic and Persian.

Seleucus and his successors accepted this reality. They also saw the wisdom of maintaining other aspects of traditional Mesopotamian culture to make running such a large, diverse state more manageable. For example, they retained most of the old Persian administrative system. The Seleucids also recognized the traditional Mesopotamian gods and faithfully supported local temples and religious rituals. Typical was Seleucus's son, Antiochus I (reigned 281–260 B.C.). He took part in public worship of various Babylonian deities, including the chief god, Marduk, and Nabu, god of the written word. The following inscription dedicated to Nabu by Antiochus imitates the highly formalized style and tone of earlier non-Greek Mesopotamian versions:

The foundation of Ezida, the true temple, the house of Nabu, which is in [the town of] Borsippa, I did lay. O Nabu, lofty son [of Marduk], wise one of the gods . . . regard [me] joyfully and, at your lofty

Snobbery in Seleucid Society

A leading scholar of ancient times explains some of the classist aspects of society in Mesopotamia and other parts of the Near East under Greek Seleucid rule.

Socially and economically, Greek [social] elements formed a dominant level over great masses of [non-Greek] natives. [In] the great Babylonian center of Seleucia-on-the-Tigris [and Babylon] alike, groups of relatively few Greeks constituted an upper crust [in society] much as did the English masters of Bombay, Singapore, or Hong Kong in the nineteenth century. Culturally [speaking], these Greeks clung to their ancestral inheritance, though they were willing to admit wealthier natives to their ranks so long as these men Hellenized themselves [adopted Greek language and customs].

Chester G. Starr, *A History of the Ancient World*. New York: Oxford University Press, 1991, p. 408.

This clay seal depicts a priest praying before the symbols for Marduk, chief god of Babylon, and Nabu, god of the written word. Seleucia-on-the-Tigris became a main trade hub and pulled business and people away from Babylon, causing the decline of the city.

command which is unchanging, may the overthrow of the countries of my enemies . . . just kingship, [and] a happy reign . . . be [your] gift for the kingship of Antiochus . . . forever.[45]

Seleucid Cities and Commercial Centers

Because Greek culture and administrative control was strongest in the region's urban centers, the Seleucid rulers devoted much of their considerable wealth to building and maintaining cities. Seleucus alone established dozens of towns and cities across Mesopotamia and neighboring regions. According to Libanius, a later Greek writer who grew up in one of the greatest of these cities, Antioch, on Syria's Mediterranean coast:

> The other [Near Eastern] kings have [taken pride] in destroying cities. He [Seleucus], on the other hand, arranged to build cities that did not yet exist. . . . One can go to Phoenicia to see his cities, one can go to Syria and see even more and greater cities of his. He extended this noble work up to the Euphrates and Tigris. And surrounding Babylon with cities, he scattered them everywhere, even in Persia [here meaning Iran]. In short, there was no place suitable to receive a city that he left bare.[46]

Several of the Seleucid cities became thriving centers of trade and commerce. One, the imperial capital—Seleucia-on-the-Tigris, situated a few miles northeast of Babylon—became the main hub of all the major trade routes that passed through Mesopotamia. The new city steadily pulled both residents and business away from Babylon, sending that ancient metropolis into decline. Still, Mesopotamia was extremely productive and enjoyed considerable economic prosperity. Under Seleucid rule, noted scholar Michael Grant writes, Mesopotamia's

great potential fertility was exploited by efficient irrigation, its . . . industry flourished, and trading and banking reached a high degree of development. . . . Much of this prosperity was due to Seleucia-on-the-Tigris. . . . [It] was a river port for maritime shipping, linked with settlements on the Persian Gulf . . . where vessels from southern Arabia and India called on their way up the Tigris. But Seleucia was also the center upon which all the main land-routes converged. . . . Few places have ever so effectively dominated the business affairs of half a continent.[47]

Decline of the Seleucids

If the Seleucid rulers had remained in power long enough, they might eventually have transformed Mesopotamia into an extension of Greece—and therefore a Western-based cultural region. In that case, the later history of both the Near East and Europe would have been very different. However, their empire, like those of the Persians and Medes before them, turned out to be relatively short-lived.

The decline of the Seleucid realm resulted from several factors. First, despite the best efforts of those in charge, it was simply too big, spread out, and complex to manage effectively on an indefinite basis. The Seleucids always faced an uphill battle, scholar Peter Green explains, in part because "they did not control one well-defined and well-protected area, unified ethnically and virtually safe from invasion. What they had was a loose, [ethnically diverse] mass of old Persian satrapies, where communications were, at the best of times, hazardous. . . . [For example] the Seleucids never controlled the royal road from Susa to Sardis for all its length."[48]

Also, the quality of leadership among the Seleucid rulers deteriorated steadily over time. The empire's founder and some of his immediate successors were capable rulers. But the later ones, in Green's words, were "selfish, greedy, murderous, weak, stupid, vicious, sensual, vengeful, and . . . suffer[ed] from the effects of prolonged inbreeding. . . . [They possessed] no long-term economic insight [and aimed] at little more than immediate profits and dynastic self-perpetuation."[49]

Making matters worse, the Seleucid rulers fought numerous wars with enemies who frequently pressed at and chipped away at their borders, activities that wasted valuable human and material resources. In the west, the Seleucids battled other Hellenistic realms, especially Ptolemaic Egypt. These struggles ended in a huge battle at Raphia, in southern Palestine, in 217 B.C. Ptolemy IV soundly defeated the Seleucid king Antiochus III (222–187 B.C.), who lost some ten thousand men killed and four thousand captured. Antiochus also lost much western territory to the Romans, masters of the Italian peninsula, who were beginning to make inroads into the near East. In

190 B.C., at Magnesia-ad-Sipylum (in Anatolia), they slew more than fifty thousand of his troops. According to a later Greek writer, Appian of Alexandria, when Antiochus "saw the field of battle strewn with the bodies of his

This stone tablet from the Seleucid period outlines the daily rituals regarding sacrifices at the temple of the god Anu in Uruk.

Antiochus Versus the Romans

The Seleucid monarch Antiochus III fared badly against the Romans, who themselves, like him, would later briefly control Mesopotamia. In 192 B.C., he responded to a call from some mainland Greeks who wanted to rid their land of Roman intruders and arrived in Greece with 10,000 soldiers. The following year, a Roman force of 20,000 men attacked Antiochus in the pass of Thermopylae (in central Greece). Seeing the enemy approaching, the Seleucid troops panicked. "Such sudden terror gripped them all," the Roman historian Livy recalled, "that they cast away their arms and fled." Of Antiochus's forces, "the only men to escape were the 500 who accompanied the king," who managed to escape. Later, the Romans delivered Antiochus an even larger and more humiliating defeat. At Magnesia-ad-Sipylum, in Anatolia, he lost more than

Antiochus III was repeatedly defeated by the Romans.

50,000 soldiers, compared to only 350 Romans killed.

Livy, *History of Rome,* books 31–45 published as *Livy: Rome and the Mediterranean,* trans. Henry Bettenson. New York: Penguin, 1976, pp. 256–257.

own men, horses, and elephants, and his camp already captured, he fled . . . arriving at Sardis [in western Anatolia] about midnight. From Sardis . . . on the following day he retreated to Syria, leaving [some of his] officers . . . to collect the remains of his army."[50] Antiochus's defeat was so enormous that it allowed the Romans to seize outright all of the Seleucid holdings in Anatolia.

A Relentless Foe

On the eastern side of their empire, meanwhile, the Seleucid monarchs faced a foe no less fearsome and relentless than the Romans. In 238 B.C., the Parthians, a band of nomadic Iranian tribesmen, took control of large portions of the former Persian satrapy lying southeast of the Caspian Sea. The reigning Seleucid king, Seleucus II (ca. 246–225 B.C.), was preoccupied with internal power struggles and other problems and did little to check Parthian expansion. That expansion continued. And in 141 B.C. the Parthians managed to seize Mesopotamia.

The much-reduced Seleucid realm, now centered in Syria, continued to exist a while longer. But without the lucrative agricultural lands, trade routes, and thriving cities of the Mesopotamian plains, the Greeks no longer had a viable economic base in the area. Large numbers of Greek farmers, merchants, and artisans still resided on these plains. But like so many others before them, they steadily merged into the rich local melting pot of peoples, who now had to do the bidding of still another line of ambitious tyrants who believed they were destined to rule forever.

Chapter Seven

ANCIENT MESOPOTAMIA'S LAST EMPIRES

After the Greek Seleucids lost control of Mesopotamia in 141 B.C., the region came under Parthian rule, a state of affairs that endured for almost four centuries. Indeed, the Parthians were remarkably successful in the area. Their empire lasted considerably longer than those of Sargon the Akkadian, Ur-Nammu the Sumerian, Cyaxares the Mede, Cyrus the Persian, and Seleucus the Macedonian Greek.

Yet considering the longevity of Parthian rule in Mesopotamia and Iran, relatively little of a substantial nature is known about Parthian leaders, politics, internal affairs, and customs. The main reason is a lack of surviving written records from Parthia itself. As scholar John Curtis of the British Museum says, "Unfortunately, practically nothing the Parthians might have written about themselves has been preserved." Therefore, "for historical information about the Parthians we are largely dependent on the works of Greek and Latin [Roman] authors."[51]

Because the Greeks and Romans viewed the Parthians as enemies and inferiors, their accounts are naturally biased. Nevertheless, some of these writings do provide valuable insights about the Parthians, including how their armies maneuvered and fought on the battlefield. A notable example is the first-century-A.D. Greek biographer Plutarch's detailed account of the battle of Carrhae. Fought in northeastern Mesopotamia in 53 B.C., it pitted a Parthian army against a large force of invading Romans.

Some two centuries later, the Parthians faced another formidable enemy. One of their leading subjects rebelled, overcame them, and established a new large-scale realm in the region—the Sassanian Empire. This state, too, lasted for about four centuries.

More is known about Sassanian rulers and society than about their Parthian counterparts. In addition to a few surviving Sassanian writings, there are numerous surviving rock carvings, inscriptions, mosaics, paintings, and assorted arts and crafts. This array of evidence has allowed modern scholars to piece together an incomplete, though reasonably clear, picture of Sassanian history and society. As it turned out, several elements of Sassanian art and culture also survived in a different manner. These elements were absorbed by the Arab Muslims, whose conquest of the Sassanian realm in the A.D. 600s brought Mesopotamia's ancient era to a close.

Rise of the Parthians

Today, some experts view the Parthians and Sassanians as latter-day Persians (or neo-Persians) because their royal dynasties were, like the one Cyrus established, rooted in Iran. Indeed, the Parthians emerged from the region lying southeast of the Caspian Sea, now in northeastern Iran. Their ancestors probably migrated there from farther north, in south-central Asia. This had long been a Persian province, called Parthava. But then Alexander the Great incorporated it into his own empire, and not long afterward, the Seleucids claimed ownership of Parthava. They were able to maintain only marginal control over the area, however. So over time, local Parthian leaders began to assert themselves, and the region became increasingly independent.

The most influential of these local leaders was Arsaces, who proclaimed himself king of the Parthian tribes in 247 B.C. This marked the inception of the Arsacid dynasty of Parthian rulers. Nine years later, Arsaces defeated Parthava's Seleucid satrap, Andragoras, in battle, which solidified Parthian control of what is now northern Iran.

Thereafter, the Seleucids steadily lost territory to the ambitious Parthians. Not long after 200 B.C., one of Arsaces' successors seized control of the Silk Road, an important trade route running through

A silver vase is shown here from the Sassanian era. The Sassanian Empire lasted for about four centuries.

An Eerie, Terrifying Sound

In his vivid description of the battle of Carrhae (in his biography of Marcus Licinius Crassus), Plutarch included the following account of the large drums the Parthians used to unnerve their enemies on the battlefield.

The whole plain was filled with a deep and terrifying roaring sound. For the Parthians, instead of having horns or trumpets to sound the attack, made use of hollow drums of stretched hide to which bronze bells were attached. They beat on these drums all at once in many different parts of the field and the sound produced is most eerie and terrifying, like the roaring of wild animals with something of the sharpness of a peal of thunder. They have, it seems, correctly observed that the sense of hearing has the most disturbing effect on us of all our senses, most quickly arouses our emotions, and most effectively overpowers our judgment.

Plutarch, *Life of Crassus*, in *Fall of the Roman Republic: Six Lives By Plutarch*. Trans. Rex Warner. New York: Penguin, 2006, p. 142.

Mesopotamia, southern Iran, and farther eastward to India and China. This both hastened the Seleucid realm's decline and contributed to Parthia's rising wealth and power.

The greatest prize of all for the Parthians was Mesopotamia and its fertile, populous river valley. In 141 B.C., the Parthian king Mithridates I (reigned 171–ca. 138 B.C.) captured most of the area, including its two principal cities, Seleucia-on-the-Tigris and Babylon. The Parthians then erected a new capital city of their own—Ctesiphon, near the junction of the Tigris and Diyala rivers.

Parthian Society and Rule

The Parthians had proved themselves to be effective fighters and determined conquerors. However, before carving out their empire, they apparently had been considerably less culturally advanced than their predecessors in Mesopotamia, especially the Babylonians, Persians, and Greeks. Recognizing this culture gap, the Parthian kings tolerated and absorbed, rather than suppressed, existing customs and beliefs in the region. Indeed, these rulers came particularly to admire Greek culture and placed many local Greeks in Parthian government jobs. "In the early part of the Parthian period, Greek was retained as the official language," Curtis states. "Greek cities such as Seleucia [on-the-Tigris] were allowed to prosper, and Mithridates and some of his successors used the [term] "Philhellene" ["admirer of the Greeks"] on their coins. The art of this early period also shows marked

A Parthian rhyton (a container for holding liquid) is shown here. During this period, drinking horns were mainly decorated with Greek mythological scenes or characters.

[Greek] influence . . . [as] seen on [Parthian] drinking horns [that] are mainly decorated with Greek mythological scenes."[52] This marked preference for and promotion of Greek traditions stimulated the growth of a sort of Greco-Iranian culture in Mesopotamia and southern Iran. One result was that the practice of Persian traditions, including religious ones, slowly declined in these areas.

The Parthians also lacked the strong, central administrative organization of earlier Mesopotamian-based empires. This was not because of a lack of vision and talent, but rather personal preference based on long-standing Parthian tradition. It appears that the Parthians had originated as separate nomadic tribes. Though all were related by language and culture, each had a certain amount of autonomy, or self-government. Retaining this social-political structure, the Parthian Empire became a kind of feudal state in which several strong, independent vassal lords or chiefs swore allegiance to the strongest of their number. He bore the title of king.

This explains why there was no overall, national Parthian army. Instead, each chief commanded a small but effective army of his own, and when necessary two or more of these local armies came together and supported the king's own personal forces. Similarly, the local chiefs oversaw the management of their own subregions. "Within these regions," Norman Hunt explains, "local leaders and administrators were left unmolested by central authorities. Taxes were imposed, but these were seen to be fair and just, and there is no record that the Parthians interfered in local politics to any great extent. People were free to follow a regional leader or to honor a diverse range of local [traditional Mesopotamian] deities."[53]

Parthia Versus Rome

A major test for the strength and durability of this loose political structure came in 53 B.C., when the Romans invaded Mesopotamia. Marcus Licinius Crassus, a wealthy businessman and governor of Rome's province of Syria, sought to conquer Parthia and make it part of the growing Roman realm. Hearing of the Roman advance, the Parthian king, Orodes II, wasted no time. He dispatched one of his regional chiefs, Spahbod Surena, who hurried westward with a small army of ten thousand horse soldiers. (The Parthians were renowned for their cavalry, consisting of a mix of armored knights and highly mobile mounted archers.) Plutarch summed up Orodes' probable strategy this way: "He took the danger very seriously and was holding himself [and larger groups of Parthian soldiers] in reserve, waiting to see what would happen, meanwhile sending Surena forward to test the enemy forces in battle and to interfere with their movements."[54]

Surena and his troops clashed with Crassus and his larger army of thirty-five thousand infantry and cavalry near Carrhae (situated a few miles east of the Euphrates River). Crassus's men were exhausted from a long march through

A Roman sculpture of a wounded Parthian general on horseback. The Parthian army was renowned for its cavalry.

arid territory. He unwisely refused to make camp and let them rest before the battle. That mistake, coupled with Surena's superior generalship, proved disastrous for the Romans, who were subjected for hours to a merciless, lethal rain of Parthian arrows. "There was no attempt at accurate marksmanship," Plutarch recalled, "since the Romans were so densely crowded together that it was impossible to miss the target even if one wished to do so."[55]

The end results were catastrophic for the Romans. Some twenty thousand of them were killed, including four thousand wounded men butchered by the Parthians after the battle was over. Another ten thousand Romans were captured. Crassus himself was slain a few days later during a peace negotiation with Surena. In addition to the great cost in lost life, the Romans suffered what was to them the enormous humiliation of having their proud battle flags seized by the enemy.

For these reasons, the Romans long held a grudge against Parthia. And nearly two centuries elapsed before they achieved what they viewed as justice. In A.D. 116, the emperor Trajan launched a massive invasion of Mesopotamia and sacked Ctesiphon. Two generations later, another Roman ruler, Marcus Aurelius, also successfully invaded Mesopotamia, and one of his immediate successors, Septimius Severus, did the same. The latter emperor's soldiers looted Ctesiphon and large tracts of territory surrounding it.

Rise of the Sassanians

These destructive attacks severely crippled the Parthian realm. And as had happened so often in the past, ambitious individuals with armies at their disposal saw a situation that might be exploited. As Hunt explains: "The Parthian-Roman wars weakened the central dynasty's hold on the resources and manpower they needed to maintain their position [and] some provincial [leaders became] strong enough to threaten the dynasty."[56]

In 224, one of these regional leaders, Ardashir, who ruled the old Persian heartland of Fars, challenged the badly weakened Parthian king, Artabanus IV. Their armies met, and Ardashir was the victor. Afterward, he spent the next few years battling and absorbing those Parthian regions that he did not already control.

Ardashir established a new dynasty and empire in the region—the Sassanian (or Sassanid), named for his grandfather, Sassan, who had been a highly influential priest and political leader in Fars. Sassan had strongly promoted the old Persian religion Zoroastrianism. He had also called for reestablishing other aspects of traditional Persian culture. Ardashir heeded this call. He and his successors identified themselves as "Mazda-worshiping kings," in reference to the chief Persian god, Ahura-Mazda. The Sassanian rulers also revived Persian social customs and political practices. They established a central imperial government in Ctesiphon, which they rebuilt and expanded. And they maintained a strong national army whose soldiers answered to the king rather than to regional leaders.

The Romans viewed the rise of this powerful new Near Eastern state as ominous. They were particularly disturbed when Ardashir's son, Shapur I (reigned 241–272), launched raids into Roman territories in Anatolia, Syria, and Armenia. Bent on retaliation, the Roman emperor Valerian personally oversaw a military campaign in the Near East. But Shapur eventually defeated him. After the battle, the two leaders met to negotiate peace, but the Sassanian king took his opponent prisoner and Valerian spent the rest of his life in the humiliating role of Shapur's personal servant. According to the third-century-A.D. Latin writer Lactantius:

> [Valerian] wasted the remainder of his days in the vilest condition of slavery. Shapur, the king of the [Sassanians], who had made him prisoner, whenever he chose to get into his carriage or to mount on horseback, commanded the Roman to stoop and present his back, then [set] his foot on the shoulders of Valerian [thereby using him as a human stool]. Valerian lived for a considerable time under the . . . insults of his conqueror. . . . Afterward, when he had finished this shameful life under so great dishonor, he was flayed [sliced up], and his skin, stripped from the flesh, was dyed with vermilion [bright red], and placed [on public display] in [a Sassanian] temple.[57]

Ardashir established the Sassanian empire and promoted Zoroastrianism, the old Persian religion. Pictured here is a relief sculpture of the Zoroastrian god Ahura-Mazda.

The Legendary Sassan

Ardashir's grandfather, Sassan, became a larger-than-life figure among the Parthians, as Gilgamesh had among the Sumerians and Cyrus had among the Persians. Consequently, numerous fanciful legends grew up about Sassan in later ages; modern scholars have a difficult time trying to determine who he really was and what he actually did. One legend, preserved in a late Sassanian text, claims that Ardashir's father, Papag, dreamed that Sassan would be reincarnated in the young Ardashir, who would rule the world.

Ardashir was the son of Papag and the grandson of Sassan.

One night Papag saw in a dream as though the sun was shining from the head of Sassan and giving light to the whole world. Another night he dreamed that Sassan was seated on a richly adorned white elephant, and that all those that stood around him in the kingdom . . . praised and blessed him. . . . [Priests] told Papag: "The person that was seen in that dream . . . will succeed to the [rule] of this world [through a descendant]."

Darab Dastur Peshotan Sanjana, trans., "Book of the Deeds of Ardashir Son of Babag," Avesta—Zoroastrian Archives. www.avesta.org/pahlavi/karname.htm.

The Sassanians' Decline and Fall

In the years that followed, the Sassanians continued to expand their realm. In the east, it encompassed what is now Afghanistan and reached the Indus River, in western India. And in the west, one Sassanian monarch, Khusrau II (590–628), seized sections of Syria, Palestine, and Egypt, though these areas did not remain in the empire for long.

Over time, however, the Sassanian rulers encountered the same dilemma that so many other Near Eastern imperialists had in prior ages. Namely, ruling such a vast realm inhabited by diverse peoples was extremely expensive and difficult. They ended up allocating much of their time, money, and energy on the upkeep of their heartland, in southern Iran. In consequence, Mesopotamia fell into neglect. Many of its towns that had been damaged or destroyed during centuries of wars among Parthians, Sassanians, and Romans were never rebuilt. Meanwhile, thousands of irrigation canals, which had for millennia brought life-giving water to local urban populations, fell into disrepair and disappeared beneath the increasingly arid earth.

In retrospect, it is not surprising that this long-term neglect of Mesopotamia left it open to abuse by an outside power. Sure enough, the Byzantines (former eastern Romans who had created an empire centered in Greece and Anatolia) invaded Mesopotamia in 628 and sacked Ctesiphon. King Khusrau hastened to drive back the intruders. But some of his own followers killed him, while the rest of the army rebelled.

In the following few years, six different rulers sat on the Sassanian throne. All were weak and allowed the empire

During Sassanian rule, many Mesopotamian towns fell into neglect. Many of them had been damaged or destroyed during centuries of wars among Parthians, Sassanians, and Romans. Shown here are the ruins of the Palace of Shapur I.

to lapse into a decentralized state like Parthia in its own final years. Making matters worse, the last of these monarchs, Yazdgard III, witnessed the appearance of a formidable new enemy. Led by a capable general named Khalid Ibn al-Walid, an army of Muslim Arabs swept into southern Mesopotamia and captured Ctesiphon. The Parthian king fled eastward in such a hurry that he left behind his treasury, which fell into the invaders' hands. Not long afterward, a few of Yazdgard's local governors banded together and in 641 made a last stand against the Arabs. But this effort proved useless. The governors went down to defeat, and the Sassanian realm ceased to exist. Yazdgard survived in exile in what is now Afghanistan until 651, when a local peasant murdered him.

A Collective Heritage

By the time of Yazdgard's death, all of Mesopotamia and Iran, along with Syria-Palestine, had come under Arab control. The new rulers made Arabic the official language and their recently adopted faith—Islam—the state religion. Modern scholars view the Muslim era that now ensued for several centuries as part of Mesopotamia's medieval period. Therefore, the fall of the Sassanian dynasty marked the close of the region's ancient era.

Yet some of the religious, social, and artistic ideas and customs practiced by the wide array of peoples who had lived in Mesopotamia remained intact. As Hunt says, "Although different civilizations flourished and waned throughout the long period of Mesopotamian

The Origins of Islam

The Arabs who overran the Sassanian Empire in the A.D. 630s were Muslims, having converted to the new faith of Islam shortly before. Their holy prophet, Muhammad, had been born a boy named al-Amin (meaning "the Faithful") at Mecca, in western Arabia, circa 571. When he was a young man, he worked as a merchant. But then, according to the faithful, he was blessed with a visit by the angel Gabriel. The words

Gabriel spoke to the young man became the basis of Islam's holy book, the Koran. The people of Mecca persecuted al-Amin. So he journeyed to Medina, north of Mecca, where he took the name Muhammad and acquired many converts to the principles of the Koran. Islam then spread to Mecca, other parts of Arabia, and not long afterward beyond Arabia's borders into Mesopotamia and other Near Eastern regions.

history . . . there had been a continuity in cultural identity."[58] That is, over the ages each group that had settled in the area had to some degree adapted to existing customs and beliefs, while adding their own cultural traits into the mix. Thus, for instance, the last major ancient Mesopotamian people, the Sassanians, profoundly shaped the culture of their conquerors. "Sassanian influence is everywhere to be seen in Islamic art," Curtis points out, including "the standard mosque plan derived from the Sassanian [dome]."[59] In this and countless other ways, the collective heritage of ancient Mesopotamia's peoples and empires passed, often subtly and silently, into the larger melting pot of peoples and nations making up the modern world.

Notes

Introduction: On Civilization's Cutting Edge

1. Samuel N. Kramer, *Cradle of Civilization.* New York: Time-Life, 1978, p. 11.
2. Kramer, *Cradle of Civilization,* pp. 11, 159–160.
3. Stephen Bertman, *Handbook to Life in Ancient Mesopotamia.* New York: Facts On File, 2003, p. 63.

Chapter One: The First Farmers and City Dwellers

4. Norman B. Hunt, *Historical Atlas of Ancient Mesopotamia.* New York: Facts On File, 2004, p. 10.
5. Hunt, *Historical Atlas of Ancient Mesopotamia,* p. 15.
6. Karen R. Nemet-Nejat, *Daily Life in Ancient Mesopotamia.* Peabody, MA: Hendrickson, 2002, p. 14.
7. Nemet-Nejat, *Daily Life in Ancient Mesopotamia,* p. 14.
8. Quoted in Kramer, *Cradle of Civilization,* p. 127.
9. Bertman, *Handbook to Life in Ancient Mesopotamia,* p. 191.
10. Kramer, *Cradle of Civilization,* p. 34.

Chapter Two: Rise and Fall of the Earliest Empires

11. Bertman, *Handbook to Life in Ancient Mesopotamia,* pp. 65–66.

12. Christon I. Archer et al., *World History of Warfare.* Lincoln: University of Nebraska Press, 2002, p. 5.
13. Gwendolyn Leick, *The Babylonians.* London: Routledge, 2003, p. 27.
14. Quoted in Electronic Text Corpus of Sumerian Literature, "Death of Ur-Nammu." http://etcsl.orinst.ox.ac.uk/cgi-bin/etcsl.cgi?text=t.2.4.1.1&charenc=j#.
15. Quoted in Thorkild Jacobson, *The Treasures of Darkness: A History of Mesopotamian Religion.* New Haven: Yale University Press, 1978, pp. 87–89.
16. Leick, *The Babylonians,* p. 29.
17. Leick, *The Babylonians,* p. 28.

Chapter Three: Babylonia, Assyria, and Their Rivals

18. Leick, *The Babylonians,* p. 33.
19. Quoted in Jorgen Laessoe, *People of Ancient Assyria: Their Inscriptions and Correspondence,* trans. F.S. Leigh-Browne. London: Routledge and Kegan Paul, 1963, p. 43.
20. Quoted in Daniel D. Luckenbill, ed., *Ancient Records of Assyria and Babylonia,* vol. 1. New York: Greenwood, 1989, p. 17.
21. Leick, *The Babylonians,* p. 37.
22. Nemet-Nejat, *Daily Life in Ancient Mesopotamia,* p. 31.
23. Quoted in Robert F. Harper, *The Code of Hammurabi.* Chicago: University of Chicago Press, 2007, pp. 195–97.

Chapter Four: A Ruthless Spirit: The Neo-Assyrians

24. Kramer, *Cradle of Civilization,* p. 59.
25. Chester G. Starr, *A History of the Ancient World.* New York: Oxford University Press, 1991, p. 133.
26. Georges Roux, *Ancient Iraq.* New York: Penguin, 1993, p. 264.
27. Starr, *A History of the Ancient World,* p. 133.
28. Quoted in Luckenbill, *Ancient Records of Assyria and Babylonia,* vol. 1, p. 110.
29. Quoted in Luckenbill, *Ancient Records of Assyria and Babylonia,* vol. 1, pp. 166–67.
30. 2 Kings 15:29.
31. Quoted in Luckenbill, *Ancient Records of Assyria and Babylonia,* vol. 2, p. 152.
32. Quoted in Luckenbill, *Ancient Records of Assyria and Babylonia,* vol. 2, p. 234.
33. Quoted in Luckenbill, *Ancient Records of Assyria and Babylonia,* vol. 2, p. 293.
34. Nahum 2:1–10.
35. The saying comes from the Bible. Galatians 6:7 states: "Whatsoever a man sows, that will he reap," meaning that what one does in life will eventually come back to reward or punish him or her. Eastern religions call it the law of karma.

Chapter Five: Triumph and Tragedy: The Persian Empire

36. Tom Holland, *Persian Fire: The First World Empire and the Battle for the West.* New York: Doubleday, 2005, pp. xviii–xix.
37. Herodotus, *The Histories,* trans. Aubrey de Sélincourt. New York: Penguin, 2003, p. 84.
38. Herodotus, *Histories,* p. 94.
39. Herodotus, *Histories,* p. 95.
40. Quoted in A.T. Olmstead, *History of the Persian Empire.* Chicago: University of Chicago Press, 1966, p. 51.
41. Herodotus, *Histories,* pp. 369–70.

Chapter Six: Greek Attempts to Rule Mesopotamia

42. Quoted in Kenneth J. Atchity, ed., *The Classical Greek Reader.* New York: Oxford University Press, 1996, pp. 182–83.
43. Arrian, *Anabasis Alexandri,* published as *The Campaigns of Alexander,* trans. Aubrey de Sélincourt. New York: Penguin, 1986, pp. 119–120.
44. Hunt, *Historical Atlas of Ancient Mesopotamia,* p. 152.
45. Quoted in James B. Pritchard, ed., *Ancient Near Eastern Texts Relating to the Old Testament.* Princeton: Princeton University Press, 1992, p. 317.
46. Quoted in Graham Shipley, *The Greek World After Alexander, 323–30 B.C.* London: Routledge, 2000, p. 304.
47. Michael Grant, *From Alexander to Cleopatra: The Hellenistic World.* New York: Charles Scribner's Sons, 2000, pp. 59–60.
48. Peter Green, *Alexander to Actium: The Historical Evolution of the Hellenistic*

Age. Berkeley and Los Angeles: University of California Press, 1993, pp. 194–95.

49. Green, *Alexander to Actium,* pp. 554–55.

50. Appian, *The Syrian Wars,* trans. Horace White, excerpted in Livius Articles on Ancient History. www.livius.org/ap-ark/appian/appian_syriaca_08.html#.

Chapter Seven: Ancient Mesopotamia's Last Empires

51. John Curtis, *Ancient Persia.* Cambridge, MA: Harvard University Press, 1990, p. 58.

52. Curtis, *Ancient Persia,* p. 59.

53. Hunt, *Historical Atlas of Ancient Mesopotamia,* p. 156.

54. Plutarch, *Life of Crassus, in Fall of the Roman Republic: Six Lives By Plutarch,* trans. Rex Warner. New York: Penguin, 2006, p. 139.

55. Plutarch, *Life of Crassus,* p. 143.

56. Hunt, *Historical Atlas of Ancient Mesopotamia,* p. 172.

57. Lactantius, *The Deaths of the Persecutors,* Christian Classics Ethereal Library. www.ccel.org/ccel/schaff/anf07.iii.v.v.html.

58. Hunt, *Historical Atlas of Ancient Mesopotamia,* p. 186.

59. Curtis, *Ancient Persia,* p. 69.

Time Line

B.C.

ca. 9000
Agriculture begins in the Fertile Crescent, the area lying along the northern rim of the Mesopotamian plains.

ca. 3300–3000
The Sumerians begin building the world's first cities.

ca. 2300
The first known empire, centered in north-central Mesopotamia, is established by Akkadian ruler Sargon the Great.

2112
Ur-Nammu, king of the city of Ur, founds the empire known as the Third Dynasty of Ur, or Ur-III.

2004
Ur is sacked by the Elamites, causing the collapse of Ur-III.

ca. 2000
An unknown Babylonian scribe writes a version of the famous epic poem about the early Mesopotamian hero Gilgamesh.

ca. 1813–1781
Reign of Shamshi-Adad, founder of Assyria's first royal dynasty.

ca. 1760
Hammurabi, king of Babylon, captures the kingdom of Mari, on the upper Euphrates.

ca. 1595
The Hittites, hailing from Anatolia, sack Babylon.

ca. 1365–1330
Reign of Ashur-uballit I, first major king of Assyria's second phase of expansion in Mesopotamia.

ca. 722–705
Reign of Sargon II, founder of the Sargonid dynasty, under which Assyria attains its maximum territorial extent.

ca. 668–627
Reign of the last Assyrian monarch, Ashurbanipal.

612
The Babylonians and Medes attack Assyria and sack Nineveh.

ca. 550
Cyrus II, Persia's first king, captures the Median capital of Ecbatana.

525
Cyrus's son, Cambyses, invades Egypt.

480
The Persian king Xerxes attacks Greece, whose city-states eventually repel the invaders.

334
The Macedonian Greek king Alexander the Great begins his swift conquest of the Persian Empire.

323

Alexander dies in Babylon. His leading followers soon begin fighting for control of his empire.

281

Seleucus, founder of the Seleucid Empire, centered in Mesopotamia, dies.

141

The Parthians have control of most of the former Seleucid realm, including Mesopotamia.

A.D.

224

The Sassanian leader Ardashir, hailing from southern Iran, defeats the last Parthian king.

634–651

Muslim Arab armies conquer much of Sassanian-controlled Mesopotamia and other parts of the Near East.

For More Information

Books

Enrico Ascalone, *Mesopotamia: Assyrians, Sumerians, Babylonians.* Berkeley and Los Angeles: University of California Press, 2007. A well-written and nicely illustrated overview of the major peoples of early Mesopotamia.

Stephen Bertman, *Handbook to Life in Ancient Mesopotamia.* New York: Facts On File, 2003. A fact-filled, easy-to-read guide to the region's peoples, leaders, religious beliefs and myths, social customs, languages, arts and crafts, and much more.

Paul Cartledge, *Alexander the Great: A New Life.* New York: Overlook, 2004. One of the better recent books written about Alexander and his conquests, including that of Persian-controlled Mesopotamia.

John Farndon, *Mesopotamia.* London: Dorling Kindersley, 2007. A beautifully illustrated survey of ancient Mesopotamian history and culture, suitable for readers of all ages.

Benjamin R. Foster, ed., *From Distant Days: Myths, Tales, and Poetry of Ancient Mesopotamia.* Bethesda, MD: CDL, 1995. A very readable collection of translations of ancient Mesopotamian literature.

Norman B. Hunt, *Historical Atlas of Ancient Mesopotamia.* New York: Facts On File, 2004. Contains dozens of excellent maps showing the probable extent of the many empires that covered this pivotal region.

Don Nardo, *Ancient Persia.* San Diego: Blackbirch, 2003. A colorfully illustrated overview of the subject aimed at young readers.

———, *The Assyrian Empire.* San Diego: Lucent, 1998. Covers all the major Assyrian rulers and conquests during their three periods of imperial expansion, as well as their political organization and artistic achievements.

John M. Russell, *Sennacherib's Palace Without Rival at Nineveh.* Chicago: University of Chicago Press, 1992. An excellent exploration of this once magnificent structure, including modern excavations of its ruins.

Web Sites

Ancient Mesopotamia: Archaeology (http://oi.uchicago.edu/OI/MUS/ED/TRC/MESO/archaeology.html). This site, run by the famed Oriental Institute of the University of Chicago, features several links to brief but excellent articles about ancient Mesopotamia.

The Babylonians (http://home.cfl.rr.com/crossland/AncientCivilizations/Middle_East_Civilizations/Babylonians/babylonians.html). Though brief, this synopsis of ancient

Babylonia is well written and includes some striking photos of surviving artifacts.

Cyaxares (www.livius.org/ct-cz/cyaxares/cyaxares.html). A detailed, informational synopsis of this famous king of the Medes, with many links to related topics.

Hammurabi (www.humanistictexts.org/hammurabi.htm). Contains excellent translations of many of that famous Babylonian ruler's laws.

Persia (http://ragz-international.com/persians.htm). A brief but informative overview of Persian history, with numerous links to related topics.

The Sassanians (www.livius.org/sao-sd/sassanids/sassanids.htm). An excellent overview of the major rulers and events of the Sassanian Empire.

Index

Picture Credits

About the Author

Historian and award-winning writer Don Nardo has published many books about the ancient world, including *Life in Ancient Athens, The Etruscans, Life of a Roman Gladiator, Religion in Ancient Egypt,* literary companions to the works of Homer, Sophocles, and Euripides; histories of the Assyrian and Persian empires; and Greenhaven Press's encyclopedias of ancient Greece, ancient Rome, and Greek and Roman mythology. He lives with his wife, Christine, in Massachusetts.